Learning Architectures

Building Organizational
and Individual Learning

Learning Architectures

Building Organizational and Individual Learning

Warren R. Wilhelm

GCA Press

ISBN 0-9740104-0-5

Warren@GlobalConsultAlliance.com
www.GlobalConsultAlliance.com

Printed in the United States of America.

Table of Contents

Dedication

To my wife Judy, without whose support and caring I would not have had the perseverance to complete this writing project.

Preface

Every day organizations around the world face a ubiquitous dilemma: **not enough capable, experienced leaders**. And every day those who head these organizations search for ways to develop their people into the leaders they need. Typically they don't know how to do it quickly and effectively.

The way an organization promotes and structures learning, both individual and organizational, is its "learning architecture." These architectures can be highly structured or informal, comprehensive or spotty, intensely thoughtful or casual. Organizations that pay even the slightest attention to educating their workforce have some type of learning architecture. However, when employee development is not producing the experienced workforce and strong leaders the company needs, it is time to create or restructure the organization's learning architecture. It is for the leaders, who need to develop their workforce and produce more effective leaders in a timely manner, that this book was written.

The attitude toward learning held by the leaders of an organization will usually determine the learning architecture the company develops. It is in companies where the CEO or other top leaders truly value learning that comprehensive approaches to both individual and organizational learning are seen. In true learning organizations, provision is made for learning throughout the workforce.

The authors of *Learning Architectures* have over a hundred years of combined experience in developing leaders in organizations—from business to non-profits, government to academia. They provide their ideas, experiences and insight to you—someone who is charged with the responsibility of growing and developing your organization's members as contributors and as leaders. Improving the effectiveness of your organization's workforce and developing your leaders internally will help to improve the overall capability of your organization and increase its competitiveness. This book provides industry-proven approaches to employee development that you can immediately put to use in your organization. **It is a how-to manual for building employee development systems.**

As the primary author of *Learning Architectures*, Dr. Warren Wilhelm has been engaged in developing leaders for over twenty years. His MBA and doctoral degrees in business and organizational behavior are from the Harvard Business School. He has been a full-time academic, teaching developing leaders in four graduate business schools: Harvard Business School, Thunderbird (The American Graduate School of International Management), Babson College and the University of Colorado. Perhaps more importantly, he was charged with developing leaders as an executive in two large corporations: Amoco Corporation and AlliedSignal Corporation. At Amoco, he was head of organization and management development; at AlliedSignal, Vice President of Corporate Education and Chief Learning Officer. As a consultant, he has helped scores of organizations build their learning architectures and develop their leaders. These include SBC Communications, *USA Today*, United Technologies, JP Morgan and Blue Cross Blue Shield.

From each of these experiences Dr. Wilhelm has learned different concepts and practices of leadership development. Approaches to development that work well in one setting will not necessarily work in another. It is important to be able to assess the environment and culture in which one is trying to develop leaders. Our suggestions and insights in this book will hopefully save time and prevent resources from being wasted when designing and implementing leadership development processes in your organization; processes that will work to develop leaders faster and more effectively.

Similarly, the authors who have contributed chapters to this book are extraordinarily qualified. They have enormous collective experience in building and managing systems for developing employees into successful workers and leaders. Dr. Gary Jusela earned his Ph.D. from the Yale School of Management. He has had distinguished and successful roles as Chief Learning Officer at Equiva Corporation, Cisco Systems and Lucent Technologies. These built on many years of experience in organization and executive development at Ford Motor Company and The Boeing Company. Dr. Jusela is one of the most creative and productive developers of organizational leaders in America today. He is currently Chief Learning Officer with Home Depot, Inc. and contributed Chapter 5.

Dr. William Clover has a wealth of experience developing leaders. For twenty years he taught leadership at the United States Air Force Academy in Colorado Springs, with occasional stints teaching outside the U.S. He adds to this book the perspective of teaching military leaders. Since the Air Force, he has been responsible for developing leaders in TRW Corporation and Amoco Corporation. He also spent time as the Associate Dean and Vernon W. Piper Director of Executive Programs at the John M. Olin School of Business at Washington University in St. Louis. He has been a global consultant on learning and cultures. Currently he is the Chief Learning Officer at Williams Corporation in Tulsa, Oklahoma. Dr. Clover contributed Chapter 6.

Judy Rosenblum has likewise been developing leaders for many years in several organizations. She has been a Vice President with Coopers and Lybrand, where she was responsible for the firm's operations in a major region of the United States. She was also the Chief Learning Officer for the Coca-Cola Company for several years, where she designed and implemented novel approaches to management and leadership development. She has been a highly successful consultant. Her experience in organizations large and small brings a unique perspective to the ideas presented in this book. She is currently the Chief Operating Officer at Duke Corporate Education, Inc. in Durham, North Carolina. She contributed Chapter 7.

Dr. Frank Bordonaro recently retired as Vice President and Chief Learning Officer at Prudential Financial, where he played a critical role in the transformation of this leading (and old!) organization. He was responsible for building and managing an overall learning and development architecture for Prudential, and for directing Prudential's world-class Learning Center. Prior to joining Prudential in 1997, Dr. Bordonaro was Chief Learning Officer for McDonnell Douglas Corporation in St. Louis, where he was responsible for the design and development of a similar learning center, as well as for all development and education activities. During the McDonnell Douglas merger with Boeing, he worked with top management to support the merger through a broad range of learning activities. From 1989 to 1996, he was Director of the Johnson Management Institute for Johnson Wax in Racine, Wisconsin, where he was responsible for harnessing all learning initiatives to support a strategic business vision. As an independent consultant, his clients have included Kraft Foods, Farley Industries and AlliedSignal. He spent four years in the academic ranks as an assistant professor in the Organization Behavior Program at Indiana University. He earned his Ph.D. in Social Psychology from Vanderbilt University. He now acts as an independent consultant to organizations on the subjects of strategy, learning and change. Dr. Bordonaro contributed Chapter 8.

Lawrence Solow contributed Chapter 9, which is a comprehensive exposition of the Total Learning Architecture concept. He is uniquely qualified to present these ideas. He is an expert in organizational learning, large-scale change, organization development, personal development and total quality concepts and practices. He has been a professional contributor inside corporations such as Harley-Davidson and AlliedSignal, and a consultant to organizations including Mattel Toys, the Gannett Corporation, UNICEF and SBC Communications. He is currently involved in efforts to direct and measure the capability of human resource functions to add value to the companies of which they are a part.

With our unique perspectives and experiences, we have tried to make this book on employee and leadership development as comprehensive as possible. Readers can select the environments and cultures most relevant to their own to glean ideas they might apply in their worlds. Our goal was to cover as many different situations and applications as we could. We hope we have achieved our purpose.

This book is laid out as follows:

Nowhere has so much information about leadership and employee development been collected in one place, especially information provided by recognized experts and successful practitioners. *Learning Architectures* is our attempt to present as much wisdom as we can impart to those who are responsible for the development of today's and tomorrow's employees and leaders.

Dr. Warren Wilhelm
January, 2003

Acknowledgements

The author gratefully acknowledges the valuable contributions made by the authors of Chapters 5–9, and the fertile ideas of his colleagues including Dave Ulrich, Steve Kerr, Wayne Brockbank, Julian Kaufmann, Jim Bolt, Ron Meeks, Ed Barrett, Toni Pristo and Bruce McBratney. The author would also like to thank the editor and publisher, Kathryn Clark, for her assistance and guidance in the publication of this book.

CHAPTER 1

Learning Organizations and Learning Architectures

Why Learning Matters—The Value Proposition for Continuous Learning

When World War II ended in 1945, much of the developed world's industrial capacity lay in ruins. Only in the United States was there an industrial economy capable of supplying world demand for manufactured goods. Demand for everything from automobiles to heavy equipment to electrical and electronic goods to commodities such as steel and rubber far outstripped supply. For America, it was an almost perfect commercial opportunity to supply the world with goods at healthy profits.

This demand-supply situation lasted until the 1960s. Then, as the industrialized nations continued rebuilding (many from almost a zero base, as did Japan), a new competitive landscape began to take shape. No longer did the U.S. have an essential monopoly on manufacturing. The United Kingdom and countries in Europe gradually became able to produce quality products in sufficient quantity to be significant exporters to the rest of the world. Asian nations quickly learned how to reverse-engineer products designed elsewhere, and began to produce similar products of even higher quality, at lower prices.

In the 1970s and 1980s, the world's industrial landscape was redrawn. Countries that had been only bit players until then became powers to contend with. Throughout this period, companies based in the U.S. relaxed into complacency, born of several decades of industrial dominance built not on innovation and creativity, but on the momentum developed during WW II. Such complacency would not serve these companies well as competitive arenas were redefined for the 1980s and 1990s.

One by one, products conceived in the U.S. have been exploited successfully by other countries. There are many examples of complacency that have migrated into obsolescence. One prime example is that television picture tubes are no longer produced in the U.S. Japan also took the market for photocopiers from Xerox. The VCR, invented in the U.S., became a success story of Matsushita Electric Co. and Phillips of Holland. Asian manufacturers have also taken larger and larger chunks of market share from Detroit's Big Three automakers. Scandinavian manufacturers—Ericcson of Sweden and Nokia of Finland—are gaining an ever increasing share of the world market for cell phones.

The wake-up call for American business came in the 1980s and 1990s. In a period of reinvention of American corporations led by General Electric, most companies have now realized that their competitive world has changed forever. Never again will complacency allow business success, let alone basic survival. Now the currency of business is the ability to create, innovate and *learn faster* than the competition.

Time is being compressed to an extent thought impossible even a few years ago. The useful market life of a computer chip used to be as long as two years; now it can be as little as thirty days. It used to take Detroit automakers seven years to bring a new car model from concept to the showroom floor; now it takes only four years. And the Japanese carmakers can do it in two. The half-life of a MIT engineering graduate, the time it takes before half of what they learned in school is obsolete, is now only two and a half years. And on and on. Very few industries move today at a pace that even resembles that of two decades ago (the oil industry and the railroad industry are notable exceptions).

To compete successfully today and for the years ahead, companies (and indeed organizations of all kinds) are required to move faster than their competitors. They must conceive new products and services sooner, develop innovative systems to distribute them, continually improve their quality and constantly lower their price. **The only way to accomplish all of these things is by learning new concepts and applications faster than anyone else. This is the competitive arena of the future—the learning arena. This is the competitive arena we will explore in this book.**

Organizational Learning

The Value Proposition

The value proposition for learning is relatively simple and absolutely crucial to business success. It has two major components: *individual learning* and *organizational learning.* Both are necessary; neither is sufficient by itself.

A strong case can be made for the premise that the only sustainable competitive advantage is the ability to learn faster than the competition. Continuous learning leads to enhanced *organizational capability*—the ability of an organization to create ideas faster, move information around internally faster, work together more quickly and effectively, and produce results more consistently than can its competitors.

Intellectual capital is the primary asset of many of today's organizations. Learning is the vehicle by which a firm's intellectual capital appreciates. The concept of intellectual capital was defined by the Nobel Prize-winning economist James Tobin as the market value of a company in excess of the value of its tangible assets—its plant, equipment, patents, inventory, etc. An organization's intellectual capital exists in the minds of its members, and in the ability of those minds to work together productively.

Intellectual capital appreciates when an individual in an organization learns. A collective increase in intellectual capital occurs when many members learn. As they share their knowledge and its application, the capital increase is multiplied. Now the organization is able to do things it could not do before the learning occurred. **In true learning organizations, intellectual capital increases constantly.**

Continuously increasing intellectual capital allows a company to achieve and maintain a dominant market position for its products and services. Minnesota Mining and Manufacturing (3M) relies on constant product invention and innovation to keep it at the forefront of the market. It nurtures new ideas until their viability is demonstrated. Hewlett-Packard relies on constant innovation to keep over half its revenues coming from products in existence for three years or less. GE increases productivity (the ratio of inputs to outputs) by over five percent a year by relentlessly pushing for new and better ways to do every aspect of its widely diverse businesses. Its recent use of a Six Sigma approach to improving quality and operations is a tool to force GE employees at all levels to constantly think in new ways. Microsoft purposely obsoletes its own products because it knows if it does not, a competitor will.

The value proposition for continuous learning can be expressed simply:

Individual Learning Plus Organizational Learning = Sustainable Competitive Advantage.

This value proposition is why leaning matters. No company can maintain its competitive advantage without continuous learning. When learning is absent or weak, intellectual capital depreciates, leaving the organization further and further behind in the competitive arena. A recent study conducted by consultants at McKinsey and Co. called "The War for Talent" found that high-talent individuals are drawn to companies populated by other high-talent people; companies where they can learn and develop in a challenging environment, and where they can have impact and grow themselves constantly. Companies that cannot or do not provide such a rich, nurturing soil for contributors to grow themselves gradually lose the best of their talented employees.

More will be said later about the necessity of an organization keeping its talented people. For now let us simply acknowledge that not all employees bring equal value to their employer. The loss of high-talent people causes discontinuities in operations, lower morale, a weakening of the competitive spirit and a diminution of intellectual capital for the whole organization. It is often necessary to provide special incentives to some employees in order to encourage them to stay with the organization and to constantly increase the level of their contribution and commitment. We will return later to this subject of customizing employment relationships for higher-value employees.

Useful Definitions

Throughout this book we will be using several terms related to the process of acquiring, disseminating and increasing intellectual capital. So that we are clear in our development of ideas related to learning, it is useful to define these terms.

Learning is simply an individual or organization increasing its base of knowledge, or its ability to produce a desired result. Ideas may be created, copied, adapted or enhanced. Regardless of the source, new ideas increase the intellectual capital of the firm. Created ideas spring from the mind of an individual, or the collective mind of the organization (which is no more than several individuals thinking and working together). Ideas copied from another organization may be used as is, or adapted to the fill the needs of the learning organization. Often ideas borrowed from other organizations are used as a base upon which to build better, enhanced ideas or applications.

Knowledge management consists of acquiring, retaining, diffusing and using information and experience. Knowledge can be acquired in myriad ways, all of which bring new ideas across the external boundaries of the organization to become part of the collective intelligence. Or new thinking and ideas can be produced by people inside the organization. Either way, once acquired the knowledge must be retained, not allowed to seep out and be lost. This is part of the challenge of using all the knowledge that collectively exists in the organization.

Effectively using all the knowledge a company possesses requires both *retention* and *diffusion* of that knowledge. Retention requires that the knowledge be somehow categorized and stored. Morten Hansen and Nitin Nohria of Harvard Business School, and Thomas Tierney of Bain and Company have suggested (1999) that companies manage the collection and diffusion of knowledge in two different ways: by *codification* or by *personalization*.

The codification strategy is most often chosen by firms that do many repetitions of similar projects or processes. Using information technology (computers) as the enabling device, ideas and experiences are categorized into a collecting structure and entered into a database. Anyone in the organization who needs information about any of the topic categories can then access the database to get the information quickly and easily. Codification is often used by consulting firms as their knowledge management strategy of choice.

The codification approach is efficient in that it does not require any personal interaction, which can often be difficult given how busy people's lives are and how frequently they travel. Its weakness may lie in the need for an organization's members to take the initiative to input data into the database. Busy people may not have time to do this, nor be motivated to do so because there is no immediate reward. Firms who successfully use the codification strategy have reinforced their members' motivation to contribute information to the database by adjusting their reward systems.

Organizations that choose the personalization strategy for diffusing and using data rely heavily on personal interaction among their members. The collective intelligence of the firm is stored in the minds of its individual members. Accessing this knowledge requires personal interaction between the person seeking information and those people who possess the data. It is not always easy for these conversations to take place, given the pace of organizational life and geographical dispersion of the firm's members. Still, many large corporations rely on this knowledge management strategy.

The personalization strategy also requires that information seekers have a way to know who in their organization may have the information and experience they are looking for. This requires some kind of index, or central broker, who knows who in the organization knows what. Some companies have set up a written index; others rely on a person or persons who fill the role of broker. This difficulty of accessing information is obviously a drawback of the personalization approach. Firms who use this approach do so because the information shared by personal conversations is often much richer than that acquired electronically. Discussions about how best to use data or how to customize applications can also occur, often making the information being shared even more useful.

Hansen, Nohria and Tierney (1999) point out that these two strategies for managing knowledge—codification and personalization—are almost never used exclusively by a firm. Rather, they are used in combination, with one strategy being the dominant approach. In fact, a given situation may beg for one approach over the other, which might be just the opposite for another application.

Training is a word with many different meanings. It can involve teaching people manual skills, like masonry or typing. It can also entail imparting intellectual concepts, as we all experienced in elementary and high school. In some organizations, training may cover the whole spectrum of human resource development at all levels, from supervisory training to middle management to executive and leadership development.

In this book we want to distinguish *training* from *learning*. Training for us refers to teaching people to perform repetitive tasks, or to understand processes that already exist. This is as opposed to learning, which to us means helping people to acquire facts and information that they then associate with other knowledge they possess, to create new ideas and behaviors.

Organizations need both training and learning. Training is relatively more simple and straightforward, and we will not devote much space to this topic. It is learning, in its broader meaning, which poses the greater challenge to organizations of all kinds. This book will concentrate on learning.

Learning organizations have the ability to learn constantly from their collective knowledge and experience. They review and learn continuously from their successes and failures. They value both individual and organizational learning. They also:

- Value and encourage questioning
- Encourage conversation across boundaries
- Learn from everyone—competitors, suppliers, customers, partners and all other organizations
- Value and encourage prudent risk taking
- Expect all members to grow continuously.

Work by Jick, Nason, Ulrich, Von Glinow and Yeung (1995) gives us good definitions for an organization's learning capability. They define learning capability as the ability to generate ideas with impact (add value to stakeholders), and to generalize ideas across boundaries. These boundaries may be time, vertical, horizontal, external or geographic. There are several ways to generate ideas with impact:

- Improve it (continuous improvement)
- Buy it (competence acquisition)
- Try it (experimentation)
- Adopt it (boundary spanning).

Finally, learning organizations are able to confidently take action based on what they have learned.

The way an organization promotes and structures learning, both individual and organizational, is its "learning architecture." Such architectures can be highly structured or informal, comprehensive or spotty, intensely thoughtful or casual. Any organization that pays even the slightest attention to learning has some kind of learning architecture.

The attitude toward learning held by the leaders of an organization will usually determine the kind of learning architecture it develops. In companies where the CEO or other top leaders truly value learning, comprehensive approaches to both individual and organizational learning can be seen. In other organizations, where some people value learning but this value is not necessarily shared by top leaders, much more random or spotty approaches are used. In true learning organizations, provision is made for the learning of the entire workforce.

AlliedSignal Inc., a $15 billion manufacturing company that acquired Honeywell Inc. and was renamed Honeywell International in 1999, was a good example of a learning organization. At its head was a CEO, Larry Bossidy, who strongly believed in learning for everyone in the company, and the company as a whole. Provision was made for everyone to learn continuously, from senior executives to workers on the manufacturing floor. Those involved in manufacturing learned about manufacturing technology and managing themselves and other workers. Specialized employees updated constantly the skills they needed in their specialty, whether it was finance, law or human resource management. Senior leaders and general managers continuously built their skills in business and leadership.

At AlliedSignal, all this distributed learning was woven together into an educational fabric that gave the company a distinct competitive advantage over its slower-learning rivals. The company had a Chief Learning Officer who was responsible for all corporate learning, and the diffusion of collective knowledge. Formal and informal structures were in place to insure that knowledge was easily accessible to all company employees. And all employees were expected to grow their knowledge and skills constantly. This company is an example of one with a Total Learning Architecture.

Total Learning Architectures

A *Total Learning Architecture* (*TLA*), a term coined by the author, refers to an organization's comprehensive approach to learning. It will contain formal and informal learning mechanisms for its entire workforce. Specific learning opportunities will be customized to be most relevant to each member's learning needs.

In most organizations, every member needs to know something about a core set of ideas and procedures central to the organization's functioning and success. But not all members need to know the same level of sophistication or detail about these core components. In a TLA, opportunities are provided to all members or employees to learn as much, but only as much, as they need to know about core components.

For example, in one company for which we developed a TLA, everyone needed to know something about the six major areas of company involvement: (1) strategy; (2) globalization; (3) finance; (4) customers; (5) operational excellence; and (6) personal/interpersonal skills. They were also expected to keep abreast of the latest developments in their own functional areas of expertise.

In that company's TLA, learning was delivered at five different levels, or "Bands." Leaders at the highest level, or "Band 1," learned about all six topic areas in great breadth and depth (see Figures 1 and 2). They were, for example, required to conceive and communicate strategy to the rest of the organization.

Figure 1: An Example of a Total Learning Architecture

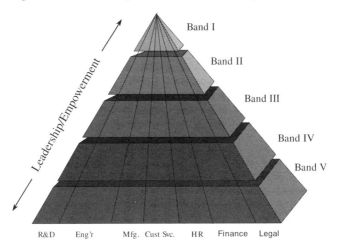

Figure 2: How the TLA Provided Selective Learning at Different Levels

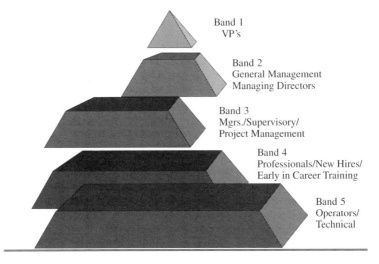

In contrast, those employees in the lowest level, Band 5, needed only to know the company's strategy, and their personal role in helping to carry it out. So the time and resources spent on strategy were much greater for Band 1, and relatively minor for employees in Band 5. On the other hand, Band 5 employees spent much more time learning about the customers with whom they interfaced daily.

Another company that has developed a highly effective TLA is General Electric. Its centerpiece is GE's renowned Crotonville leadership development center in upstate New York. At Crotonville, GE leaders participate in developmental experiences in four developmental stages:

Developmental Stage I—Leading with Ideas, Teamwork and Performance

Developmental Stage II—Creating and Leading Winning Teams and Organizations

Developmental Stage III—Improving and Integrating Key Resource Systems

Developmental Stage IV—Leading Competitive Global Businesses

GE managers return to Crotonville for learning experiences at specific times in their careers. Stage I is for leaders with 0–3 years of experience with the company. Stage II is built around first-time managers of professional employees, and for managers with several years of experience. Stage III is an integrating stage, with advanced programs in finance, human resources and information technology designed to make GE more than just the sum of its parts. The capstone courses are in Stage IV, where GE leaders are prepared to lead large, complex global organizations.

The core programs at Crotonville are only a small part of the formal learning that occurs at GE. In addition to the core, other courses and programs are offered at Crotonville that have helped GE to its current level of business success. These include training in Work-Out and Best Practices, and the highly successful GE Change

Acceleration Program. Also offered are courses in Marketing and Sales, Personal Development and GE Corporate Business Development.

In fact, however, most of the total learning in GE occurs not at Crotonville, but in GE's fifteen separate businesses. Each GE business is responsible for providing training and learning opportunities to its employees that are most relevant to that specific business. Offerings are different in each business, and at different levels within businesses. In this way, TLAs are in place within each business, and collectively they comprise a TLA for all of GE.

Many organizations aspire to having a Total Learning Architecture, but few actually achieve that goal. The first requirement is a CEO or other top leader who strongly believes in learning as a competitive advantage, and who is willing to both sponsor learning and demonstrate it by his or her continuous intellectual and experiential growth. This requirement eliminates a surprisingly large number of organizations.

The second requirement is the willingness (and ability) of an organization to support learning, both financially and with time and people resources. Some companies simply cannot spare the resources to fully support corporate learning. And other companies, which can afford to support learning and do make the commitment, sometimes fall into the trap of misdirecting their resources so that the learning that actually occurs is well below maximum effectiveness, or does not target areas most critical to the organization's success.

The third requirement for an effective TLA is the organization's ability to identify and focus on the areas of learning most critical its success, however that success may be measured. This focus requires a comprehensive diagnosis of an organization's vision, strategy, technical and human resource capability, its needed competencies for success, and an analysis of the gap between what the organization can do now and what it needs to learn.

Once the learning needs of an organization are identified, the fourth requirement comes into play. It is the ability of the organization to conceive, design and implement the kinds of learning opportunities that will produce the required learning and skills. Typically this task falls to the leadership of one person—someone who is skilled in both business and adult learning. It is the responsibility of this person, often called a Chief Learning Officer or Chief Knowledge Officer, to both identify the organization's learning needs, and put into place the means to fulfill them.

In a true sense, this person satisfies the role of a systems integrator. Once the learning needs are identified, it falls to the CLO or CKO to acquire the learning resources necessary to provide the needed learning, and to allocate those resources across the organization in the most effective and efficient manner.

The role of "learning chief" requires an almost unique person. The ideal CLO has acquired a comprehensive knowledge of business (or the primary activity in which the organization is engaged) through both formal education and personal experience. Additionally, and of equal importance, they also understand how adults learn, and have formal preparation in educational theory and pedagogy. This theoretical understanding of adult education should be bolstered by significant experience in educational design and teaching. Given all these requirements for an effective CLO, it is clear that many years of education and experience are necessary to prepare a person to successfully fill this role.

Building and maintaining a Total Learning Architecture is a critical component of any organization's competitive advantage. Those with successful TLA's have proven to outperform their competitors for years, even decades. A true learning organization will invest the time and resources necessary to construct a comprehensive Total Learning Architecture.

In the next chapter we will examine Learning Organizations in practice. Examples will be given of several organizations of all kinds that have successfully transformed themselves into true learning organizations. Readers are encouraged to steal shamelessly from the examples given and adapt the ideas for use in their own organizations.

2

Learning Organizations in Practice

Wᵉ have already discussed two examples of true learning organizations: the former AlliedSignal and General Electric. Others that can serve as models include The Drucker Foundation, Johnson & Johnson (J&J), Hewlett-Packard, Herman Miller, Colgate-Palmolive, Prudential Financial, Ford Motor Company and South Korea's LG Group.

AlliedSignal

The business success of legacy AlliedSignal serves as a measure of its capability as a learning organization. When Larry Bossidy took over as CEO in 1991, AlliedSignal was a $15 billion corporation engaged in three primary lines of business: aerospace, automotive and chemicals. It was underperforming in each of these sectors, and had little confidence from its investors that it would ever become a preeminent company. Bossidy realized that to create a more successful company would require reinvention of what he had inherited.

His chosen approach to corporate reinvention was through the vehicle of total quality. To accomplish his goal, he would have to educate 90,000 employees worldwide about the principles of total quality and the new behaviors they would all need to learn. During his first five years as CEO, he accomplished this educational feat by using 2,000 AlliedSignal employees at all levels as instructors to their 88,000 fellow workers. To simplify a much more complex challenge, history shows that Bossidy was successful in his corporate reinvention. The company was transformed from a lethargic, underperforming anachronism into a vital, exciting competitive winner that ran at warp speed.

The success of AlliedSignal was confirmed by the reaction of the investment community to its reinvention. From 1991 to 1996, the market value of the company quintupled. Bossidy created a true learning organization that in addition to teaching total quality, offered learning opportunities in scores of topic areas to employees at all levels. Learning topics included finance, operational excellence, Six Sigma quality, safety, information technology, marketing, leadership and project management. Learning was delivered by both internal and external resources with full company support.

To perpetuate his learning organization, the CEO considered commitment to continuous learning as an important factor in the evaluation of company leaders' job performance. No leader would continue to advance in AlliedSignal unless they actively supported the development of the people they led. When he retired (for the first time) in 2000, Larry Bossidy considered the creation of a learning organization as one of his most important legacies.

General Electric

General Electric is perhaps the best example of a company that has been a learning organization for over fifty years. Since the creation of GE's leadership training institute at Crotonville, New York in 1952, GE has led the way in developing leaders across its many diverse businesses. Leaders are developed in several functional specialties, including engineering, finance, marketing and sales, and human resource management. Great attention is also paid to developing general managers and corporate leaders. For decades it has been a coup for other companies to recruit leaders out of GE, because it is well known how thoroughly they have been trained.

Comprehensive learning is also offered in all of GE's fifteen businesses, which range from manufacturing of appliances to media (NBC) to finance (GE Capital). Learning opportunities are offered to employees at all organizational levels, and all employees are expected to avail themselves of these opportunities regularly.

It is this corporate-wide approach to continuous learning that has allowed GE to create what is arguably the deepest "leadership bench" in all of American business. The company literally has more leaders than it can productively use. Many of GE's best leaders leave the company to take top leadership posts at other firms. This exodus does not weaken GE, and creates more leadership opportunities for those who remain.

The Drucker Foundation

The Drucker Foundation, officially the Peter F. Drucker Foundation for Nonprofit Management, was *created* to be a learning organization. Its mission is "to lead social sector organizations toward excellence in performance" by providing social sector leaders with the resources they need to meet their challenges, and to capitalize on opportunities to innovate and change lives." Created in 1990, virtually all of the Foundation's activities focus on learning, both by the constituencies it serves and by the Foundation itself.

Under the strong direction and leadership of its Chairman Frances Hesselbein, the Foundation runs meetings and conferences, publishes books and regular newsletters, and sponsors speeches and visits all over the world. The learning focus is always the same: helping leaders in the non-and not-for-profit sectors to be more successful at achieving their goals, whatever those goals might be. These sectors have received much less learning over the years than has the private sector, yet the social sector is often the leading force in creating the major components of the world in which we all live.

The Drucker Foundation has shown that it can learn with speed and create important innovations within itself. It now takes teams of leaders and teachers to sites all over the world to spread knowledge and experience. It has over 400,000 copies of its book series in print—the Future Series of books on leadership and community. Rising to the challenges of the Internet, their website now receives thousands of visitors each month. They constantly search for and implement new ways for their constituents to learn about leadership and organizational performance. The Foundation has truly fulfilled its promise as a learning organization.

Johnson & Johnson

Healthcare company **Johnson & Johnson** (J&J) is made up of some 197 operating companies worldwide, divided into twenty-three "company groups," each with its own chairperson. The task of diffusing knowledge across the breadth of this expansive company is daunting, to say the least. Yet over the past several years, J&J has found a way to bring to bear the collective knowledge and experience of the corporation onto a wide array of problems and opportunities.

Working with the consulting firm McKinsey and Company, J&J senior executives in 1993 conceived FrameworkS, a series of focused dialogues between operating company executives, specialists and top management. The program's purpose was to foster collective thinking focused on solving a specific problem each time a FrameworkS session was convened. Topics addressed have included analyzing the changing healthcare market in the United States, the global healthcare consumer, organizational structure, operations, information management and leadership.

The FrameworkS process has allowed J&J to create new products, expand existing product lines, and even create whole new industry segments. It fosters the transfer of information throughout the silo boundaries that invariably arise in such a diverse and far-flung company. The result has been a mature company that can behave like a much younger and smaller, high-adrenalin competitor; one that has been able to both hold and increase market share in a broad array of businesses.

Hewlett-Packard

Founded in 1939 by William Hewlett and David Packard, today's technology and engineering giant **Hewlett-Packard** still has at its core the genetic code put into place by its two founders. This way of thinking and behaving has come to be known both inside and outside the company as "the H-P Way." Simply stated, the H-P Way describes a company that has great respect for its employees and their capabilities. The depth of this respect causes all the company's leaders and employees to place a high priority on continuous learning and personal development.

Because H-P's competitors move quickly and relentlessly to encroach on H-P markets and product technology, the need to learn and create constantly has always been part of the company's basic fabric. It has been company practice to hire promising college graduates and master's-degreed engineers, often in the disciplines of electrical and electronic engineering, right out of school, with the intention of developing and updating their skills constantly for their entire career (hopefully with H-P!). This "continuous learning as a way of life" quickly becomes central to the behavioral and career development expectations of H-P employees.

To avail oneself of learning opportunities both inside and outside H-P is a central part of the company's expectations of all its employees. To make this as easy as possible, learning opportunities are regularly published in print and electronically. It is the employee's responsibility to sign up for learning, in accordance with their specific learning needs. Their needs for new knowledge and skills will have been determined jointly in conversations between the employee, his or her supervisor, and representatives of the human resource department, who will add input about possible future job opportunities and career paths.

An innovation at H-P was the addition of personal computer access to learning opportunities directly from the employee's desktop. Any employee who has identified a learning need can enter their need into their PC and in return get a complete menu of learning offerings, both internal and external, which will address their need. After choosing the offering in which they wish to participate, they can sign up directly on their PC and get immediate confirmation of their participation. While it sounds simplistic, implementing this electronic learning process was complex and difficult, and ranks as a "best practice" in corporate learning systems.

Herman Miller

Herman Miller, the innovative high-quality office furniture manufacturer headquartered in Zeeland, Michigan, is a company with a long history of best practices. A growing, medium-sized company with unending aspirations to produce the best products in its chosen markets, Herman Miller is a true learning organization. Its dedication to increasing and sharing knowledge can even be seen in the physical layout of its company offices.

The company's offices are designed to encourage employees to share information at all times during the workday. Even the cafeteria has small, semi-private group seating areas to encourage people to discuss business over lunch or coffee. During hours when the cafeteria is not serving food, these seating areas are often used to conduct business. They are equipped with computer hookups for access to all electronic information sources, and are comfortable and attractive as worksites.

Several years ago the leadership of Herman Miller realized that employees needed to understand the company's business better. Profit sharing and Scanlon Plans were in place to allow all employees to share financially in the company's success, but many employees did not understand how their compensation plans worked or the formulas by which their rewards were determined. The company also began using Economic Value Added, or EVA, as way to track its performance. However, most employees did not understand this concept either.

The company initiated a large-scale learning effort, using company employees as 'teachers.' Over a period of two years, all employees learned about company operations, their compensation plans and EVA through classes presented by other Herman Miller employees. Knowing more about their company and their reward systems contributed to employees' greater commitment to the company and increased their job satisfaction, which improved performance throughout the company. These initiatives served to increase Herman Miller's dedication to continuous learning. Now new learning initiatives are introduced regularly, on the topics most important for the employees to know more about at that point in time.

Colgate-Palmolive Company

Colgate-Palmolive Company (C-P) is one of the most venerable names in American business. From its humble beginnings as a soap manufacturer, it has grown into a global presence with its products sold in 212 countries. Its 2001 sales of $9.427 billion are spread across North America, Europe, Latin America, Asia and Africa. Of its 38,500 employees, only about 6,000 are based in North America; the rest scattered over 80 countries. In 2002, it has five core businesses: Oral Care, Personal Care, Household Care, Pet Nutrition and Fabric Care. Its business strategy is simple: "Where we are the brand leader in a country, we must increase our lead; Where we are #2, we must close the gap and drive to become #1."

A cornerstone of its strategy is the growth and development of *global* leaders. As C-P drives toward its goal of "Building People Capability to Deliver Business Results," their strategy is to identify high-potentials early, assign a sequence of challenging work, provide constructive feedback and coaching, and offer continuous learning opportunities. To implement this learning strategy, four "training principles" are employed:

1. Training must be C-P-specific
2. Learners must share best practices
3. All learning must have practical work applications
4. Colgate leaders must teach

This is truly an example of learning that is directly in service of the company's business goals and objectives. Not learning "just in case," but rather learning that can and will be used the next day—just-in-time.

For example, each employee attends a program called "Valuing Colgate-Palmolive People." These programs stress C-P's global values of caring, continuous improvement and global teamwork as well as the importance of treating everyone with respect. The company's continuous growth is a direct result of having employees who live these values every day.

Prudential Financial

Prudential Financial (the former Prudential Insurance Company) exemplifies another organization that is reinventing itself, at least partially through organizational learning. When CEO Art Ryan left Chase Manhattan to take the helm of Prudential ("the Pru") in 1994, the company was in great distress. It was plagued with a rash of lawsuits stemming from the mis-selling of many of its products, and was losing market share in its most important markets. Clearly, dramatic changes had to be made if the company was to survive and prosper.

It is often difficult for a senior management team to agree on and completely understand a corporate strategy. But the more formidable task is to have all 60,000 company employees also understand the corporate strategy, and their individual role in its execution. As the Pru undertook its reinvention, that became the challenge.

To educate its entire workforce about the shifts in strategy and what would be necessary for it to succeed, Pru leadership adopted a crash approach to learning. It was built on the theory that some people learn better and more easily from graphic information than from verbal information; and used tools created by a consulting firm called Root Learning, headquartered in Perrysburg, Ohio.

The concept behind using specialized graphics to assist learning is elegantly simple. The consultants from Root Learning gathered information about the Pru, and then translated that information into four-color graphic representations of the company and its activities. Their designs pictured the configuration of the company, its various products, where money is made and spent, and perhaps most importantly, how all these pieces fit together to form a dynamic enterprise.

The graphic designs became the basis for their teaching programs, ranging in length from several hours to several days. The typical program was just one day long, and involved employees from different parts of the organization using the graphic designs to help them better understand the company, its businesses and products, and its competitive environment.

Learning sessions were facilitated by both external consultants from Root Learning, and internal Pru executives and managers. As always, one of the most significant benefits from having internal leaders do some of the teaching is that the "teachers" have to know the material better than the "students."

The use of graphic representations of its businesses is not the only example of innovative approaches to learning at Prudential. As it strives to change its strategies and culture, it must also change the way its leaders think and lead. To this end, Pru adopted a creative plan for teaching what then-CLO Dr. Frank Bordonaro called "The new skills required of leaders."

Focused on Pru's top 100 leaders, it works like this: the top 100 leaders became the internal teachers in the Root Learning one-day sessions. Each session included 200 to 300 participants, and was taught by Pru leaders with help from both internal and external consultant/facilitators. The usual configuration was to have three one-day sessions back to back, so leaders got to practice their leadership and communication skills three times in rapid succession. Leaders received preparation in advance of their sessions, and continuous coaching throughout.

The effect was to help 100 leaders learn new and more effective leadership skills in the short span of only sixteen months, and to create a critical mass of more capable leaders for the enterprise. See Chapter 8, which was written by Frank Bordonaro, ex-CLO of Prudential, for the details of this dramatic approach to leadership learning.

Ford Motor Company

At **Ford Motor Company**, a massive cultural change was undertaken, driven by a comprehensive educational effort. Called by ex-Chairman Jacques Nasser "a teachable point of view," it was intended to reinvent the way Ford employees think and behave.

All the employees of any large organization must be *aligned* in their thinking and understanding if the organization is to maximize its potential. This means that employees at all levels must understand the organization's mission, strategy and goals so that each person knows how he or she can best contribute to the organization's overall success. The teachable point of view was designed to accomplish this alignment quickly and pervasively.

The teachable point of view is "a written explanation of what a person knows and believes about what it takes to succeed in his or her own business as well as in business generally," (Tichy, 1999). "It identifies why a person approaches work as he or she does; it opens up his or her assumptions, beliefs and experiences to colleagues, bosses and subordinates."

At Ford, the teachable point of view was used to create that elusive alignment so critical to corporate success. First, Nasser and his key leaders created and wrote down their points of view, in a series of four off-site meetings over a period of four months. The process required that they discuss and debate their individual drafts to produce aligned points of view. This accomplished, these key leaders began to teach their points of view to leaders at the next level, and they to the next level, and so on. The goal was to use teaching by leaders at all levels of Ford to align the entire worldwide corporation in the shortest possible time.

The Ford approach was partly built on a foundation of learning that we have known and accepted for a very long time: that leaders who are forced to teach something learn their subject much better than they had known it before they had to teach it. In the course of preparing to teach, Ford leaders were forced to discuss and debate their own points of view. This required a deeper investigation of what each leader knows, thinks and believes than most have gone through before, so their understanding of why they act as they do is greatly enhanced. The teachable point of view thus serves another high-level purpose: it is a major vehicle for developing leaders, perhaps the CEO's most important task.

The power of the teachable point of view lies partly in its ability to cascade learning geometrically down the levels of the organization, and to do it very quickly. "Once Nasser had articulated his teachable point of view, he taught it to 200 other leaders, who taught it to 1,200 more, who taught it to 55,000 more—all within a year," (Tichy, 1999)

Nasser's use of teaching as a way to change the culture of a large organization was not new to Ford. In the early 1980s, Ford was in severe financial straits, to the point of being threatened with bankruptcy (as did happen to Chrysler Corporation). At that time, Ford mounted a massive educational effort, called TEAM, which was designed to teach all Ford employees the competitive situation the company was facing and the new approaches that would be needed to save the company. It was this initiative that made the slogan "Quality is Job One" pervasive throughout Ford.

The teaching efforts of TEAM, which encompassed the first several years of the 1980s, succeeded in not only helping to save Ford, but giving it momentum to propel it past its competitors in the U.S. auto industry, General Motors and Chrysler. Today, Ford still enjoys a residual of the momentum created by the TEAM initiative years ago. Nasser built on Ford's tradition of being a learning organization as he moved forward his initiative to once again change the Ford culture, a step he saw as critical if the company was to continue its success in markets that are rapidly reconfiguring and changing in their basic designs.

LG Group

South Korea's **LG Group** illustrates a quite different approach to corporate philosophy and the learning that ensues from that philosophy. A true learning organization, LG Group (many Americans know their products by the trade name Lucky Goldstar) has a large corporate university in Ichun City. At the university it is felt that competency-based leadership models are not very effective in developing leaders. Instead, they take a more "eastern" approach, combining business issues with philosophical and spiritual depth.

The LG approach assumes that most leaders are lonely, nervous and pressured, torn by the paradoxes of leadership, but have the potential to transform themselves. So the focus of LG's leadership development is "harmony between the harsh market and the deep mind," (Michael Lee, Deputy President, LG Academy, 1999). This approach is in contrast to that taken by many American companies, who assume the pressures of leaders' lives and essentially ignore their effects, simply taking pressure as a given.

At this writing, South Korea is emerging from serious financial and economic difficulties. The surrounding South Korean environment may be causing a temporary distortion in the learning approach espoused by LG Group; or it may not. The eastern approach described above should be revisited after South Korea rises above its current difficulties, to see if it is truly a basically different philosophical approach, or if it was temporary, a direct result of current economic problems.

Other Notable Companies

Several other companies are worthy of mention for their innovative learning practices. They are Gannett Corporation's *USA Today* newspaper unit, Texas Instruments, Campbell Soup, Equiva and SBC Communications. Not all of these companies are true learning organizations, but each has conceived an innovative and effective approach to corporate learning.

USA Today

The challenge at *USA Today* was to help bright, capable people who had typically been trained as journalists learn more about business, as the newspaper sought to increase its circulation and influence. The top 150 leaders of the company participated in a three-week learning experience designed to teach them the basics of business and how they apply to the business of *USA Today*.

The three one-week learning sessions were separated by several weeks, to allow participants to try out the new ideas to which they were being exposed. Business concepts were presented by world-class experts on each topic, who carefully tied back the intellectual content they were presenting to its possible applications in the day-to-day business of *USA Today*. The process contained a large element of action learning, in which participants worked together in small teams to solve real business problems and exploit opportunities the newspaper was facing.

The entire 150-person leadership cadre took a full year to complete the learning process, which ended in 1997. By the end of the process, a "critical mass" of leaders had been created, who thought differently and more effectively about the newspaper as a business. Partly as a result of the leaders' learning experience, in 1999 *USA Today* achieved its goal of becoming the United States' highest-circulation daily newspaper, a position it still holds in 2002.

Texas Instruments

Texas Instruments (TI) in the mid-1990s determined to essentially reinvent itself. To do so would require a new corporate strategy. The more usual approach to strategy would have the CEO craft a strategy, perhaps with the help of a few top aides; then deliver the strategy to the rest of the organization. The company chose a different, more novel approach. It broadened the strategy creation process to include many more people, in strategy teams.

The teams were composed of corporate leaders at several levels, people who were knowledgeable and capable of helping to set the company's direction for the future. Beginning in 1994, strategy teams with "rolling" membership have created or modified the strategy for TI as business conditions constantly change. The teams integrate strategy, leadership, teamwork and learning to address the key strategic issues for the company. These issues can take up to twenty-four months to address; consequently, strategy activities with the top 300+ leaders have been on a roughly annual or bi-annual basis. This is complemented by annual spring and fall strategy working sessions with the top forty managers.

The first three "strategic actions" were annual in basis. A small effort in 1994 (drafting a vision and strategy direction) was followed by larger efforts in 1995 (testing and refining their vision and strategy direction) and in 1996 (innovation and new business creation). The strategy teams used the 1996–1997 period to restructure the company's business portfolio and to complete their new business strategy on Digital Signal Processing Solutions (DSPS). In 1998 and 1999, approximately 230 people attended "Boot Camps" (very focused workshops) where focused learning was delivered on the

DSPS strategy. These 230 people sponsored another 1000 people in shortened boot camps to make sure their teams understood the issues and aligned their actions accordingly. In 2000–2002, the strategy teams focused on talent leadership. In 2002, the focus is on making customers more important.

This strategy creation process is in fact a high-level learning process. The members of the strategy teams learn how to build corporate strategy by actually doing it (action learning). As the membership of the teams changes, more people learn the strategy process. The company has now created an increasingly large cadre of senior executives who are able, based on their experience, to create strategies for the various units of the company—a much better way to learn about strategy than simply listening to experts talk about how it is done.

Campbell Soup Company

At the venerable Campbell Soup Company, as with most companies today, there was a need to build its leadership capability and to do so quickly. A new CEO had taken the reins, market conditions were changing in fundamental ways, and the company needed to bring new products to market at the same time it protected and enhanced its traditional ones.

Rather than use a "training" approach to develop promising leaders, Campbell chose to tap the power of its internal leadership resources. It had a team of ten executives who were the leadership core of the company. Each of the top ten would become a personal coach to three junior leaders for a period of ninety days.

During each ninety-day coaching period, each of the coachees would take on a project, by mutual agreement with his or her boss. The project had to be a real business problem or opportunity, with impact on the organization, the results of which could be quantitatively measured. As the coachee worked on the project during the three-month coaching period, they would have regular ninety-minute coaching sessions with their coach at two-week intervals. The job of the coach was to not only help with the problem or opportunity being targeted, but at the same time help the coachee learn about and practice effective leadership skills and behaviors.

The process included yet another learning component. During the course of the ninety-day coaching period, world-class experts would be brought in to help all the people involved in the program learn about topics relevant to their business: strategy, business acumen, organizational capability, communication, etc. For these learning sessions, the entire learning and coaching group would be brought together to learn the same things at the same time.

At the end of ninety days, the success of the projects would be assessed. Successful projects would be rewarded and less successful ones critiqued and used as case examples from which to learn. What the coachees learned about leadership would be discussed and shared among all program participants, to maximize the value of the time and resources invested in the learning process.

This innovative process was to be followed by a new round of leadership learning. The same top ten executives would each be assigned three new coachees, and the process repeated. Campbell's plans were to use this process to help create 240 more capable leaders in the short space of only two years. The faster a company can create and develop new leaders, the greater its competitive advantage.

Unfortunately, business conditions changed for Campbell Soup Company and this well-conceived process for growing leaders quickly was never implemented. It is included here because of its innovative design, which could be easily adapted to other organizations that need to develop a large number of leaders in a short time.

Equiva

Equiva is a unique story—one so compelling it is the subject of Chapter 5. Equiva is actually three companies: Equilon Enterprises LLC, Motiva Enterprises LLC and Equiva Services LLC. An alliance of the refining and marketing arms of petroleum giants Royal Dutch Shell, Texaco and Saudi Aramco, Equiva was a $42 billion startup in 1997.

Dr. Gary Jusela, Equiva's new CLO in 1998, was faced with the challenge of building the collection of disparate companies into a competitive powerhouse. Each component brought its own culture and history to the brew, and leaders often trained with very different leadership skills and styles. How to turn this massive startup into a learning organization?

The story of Equiva is told in Chapter 5, graciously contributed by Gary Jusela. It is a story of creativity in learning; people of many disciplines working together successfully and a learning design for leadership not seen before in any company.

SBC Communications

As the telecommunications industry consolidated in the 1990s, there was no more aggressive player than SBC Communications. Starting the 1990s as one of the "Baby Bells" created by the mandated breakup of the Bell System in the 1980s, SBC was originally Southwestern Bell, with a five-state presence. During the 1990s, the company renamed itself SBC Communications and went on a buying spree. It bought Pacific Bell and Nevada Bell in 1997, Southern New England Telephone in 1998 and Ameritech in 1999. By the end of the decade SBC Communications was serving the markets of 17 states.

The challenge from a learning standpoint was to find ways to integrate the leadership and employee populations of these several companies. Although they shared a common Bell System heritage, their cultures had evolved quite differently. So a learning process was designed to facilitate the building of these separate organizations into a quick-thinking, agile survivor in the brutally competitive telecommunications industry.

A two-week learning process was created to provide a vehicle for the leaders of the new organization to come together to get to know and appreciate each other, and to learn about the things most important to the company's future success. Consisting of two one-week learning sessions separated by several weeks, with classes of thirty-five to forty people each, the topics addressed included strategy, the telecommunications industry, leadership, finance, regulatory concerns, etc. Each topic was taught by a world-class expert from either inside or outside the company, or both.

The first participants in the learning process were seventy of the company's officers. At the end of the two-week learning program, they had acquired scores of new skills and knowledge directly relevant to their business, and perhaps more importantly had formed networks to allow them to work together more effectively and efficiently. A follow-up study of the learning program's effectiveness several months later showed virtually universal agreement that it had significantly shortened the time necessary to forge the company's top leadership into a competitive hammer. SBC Communications continues to be one of the most successful players as the telecom industry undergoes its metamorphosis.

In this chapter we have examined several organizations that are partly or completely Learning Organizations. Each has built a significant advantage over its competitors through appreciation of its intellectual capital, talents and skills. Each has developed partial or complete Learning Architectures, which will be discussed in greater detail in later chapters. All companies can learn from the examples provided by the companies shown here.

CHAPTER 3

New Trends in Learning and Leadership Development

From the examples presented so far, we can extract some widely-seen trends in corporate learning and leadership development. Probably the most important trend marks a key difference from the past to the present in how leadership development is pursued: **leadership development is now being combined with prosecuting the business**. There is virtually no more "just-in-case" leadership development; now it is "just-in-time."

On-Job Training

As the pace of business increased dramatically through the 1990s, and businesses have been forced to run leaner than ever before, most companies can no longer afford the luxury of taking leaders off their jobs for extended periods of time to teach them about business and leadership. Instead, leaders are learning how to be better leaders at the same time they are solving business problems and prosecuting their day-to-day responsibilities. Leadership development is now interwoven into their daily work—truly "OJT" (on-job training)—something that was once reserved for lower ranked employees.

Action Learning

Supporting this trend is the large-scale movement toward action learning. Action learning is the use of real business problems and opportunities as training grounds for executives and other leaders. As leaders work on action learning projects, they are coached and taught about the knowledge and skills necessary to successfully complete their action learning project. Coaches may be either internal or external resources, and often are both. By 2000, action learning had become the most frequently used approach to leadership development in large American corporations (survey, Executive Development Associates, 1999).

Just-in-Time Learning

Another noteworthy trend is that leadership development and business learning is now "Just-in-Time, not Just-in-Case." Learning is rarely offered today unless it can be applied the next day or the next week. The past practice of preparing leaders long before they were to take on greater responsibilities, or giving them training in skills they would not use for some time, is virtually extinct. Companies have found just-in-case learning to be too expensive in time and money.

The old AlliedSignal provides us with an excellent example of "just-in-time" learning. When CEO Larry Bossidy directed the company to make strong inroads into the China market, his executives were ill-prepared to successfully conduct business with the Chinese. Initially, teams of American executives would travel to China to set up business ventures, with the goal to get the "deal" done and declare success. The Chinese with whom they were dealing, on the other hand, were part of a culture that had existed for several thousand years. They had a very different concept of time than did the American managers. The Chinese were content to take as long as they needed to forge a satisfactory deal.

But the Americans, used to dealing with much greater speed, were eager to get the deal consummated—they often made concessions for the sake of speeding up the deal process. Only several months after the deal was done did it sometimes become clear that the deal they had struck was more advantageous to the Chinese than to AlliedSignal. After a series of these less-than-satisfactory deals, Larry Bossidy came to his learning function to ask for help in fixing the problem.

The response was to design a three and a half day workshop for AlliedSignal managers and executives to attend before they were to negotiate with the Chinese. The workshop included education about the Chinese culture and the Chinese approach to doing business. A simulated business banquet was used to acquaint the Americans with this important ritual of Chinese business. Chinese Nationals were players in the banquet simulation and spoke no English; all conversations were conducted through translators, as was usually the case in real business negotiations with the Chinese.

Small groups of five to ten Americans went through the workshop at a time. By the end of the three and a half days, the Americans were much better equipped to deal successfully with the Chinese on AlliedSignal's behalf.

This workshop exemplifies just-in-time learning. It was not conceived until there was a clear and present need for learning; the learning was specific to the problem being addressed; it took only ninety days from the time of Bossidy's request for help until the first pilot of the workshop; and it was both designed and delivered at very low cost—$30,000 for design, and only $25,000-$30,000 for each delivery, depending on the number of participants. True just-in-time learning.

Reducing the Cost of Learning

Reducing the cost of learning is another widespread trend. Here costs are calculated in both money and time. Time off the job is now often simply too expensive for busy leaders. The financial cost of learning has also come under greater scrutiny and pressure. It is now necessary to be able to show a direct link between money spent on learning and business results, as in the AlliedSignal/Chinese workshop example.

A by-product of the tightening of learning budgets has often been the reduction or elimination of internal "training" departments and full-time trainers. It is virtually impossible to keep trainers fully occupied as trainers. A good utilization rate of trainers' time may be as low as only 60%. Many companies have found it more cost-efficient to outsource their training function, using (and paying) professional trainers only for the time they actually deliver training. Companies that used to have large internal training departments may now have only a Chief Learning Officer who determines when learning is needed, and outsources exactly the training called for.

Today, learning is more often being used to change culture and mindset in companies. The realization that large-scale learning efforts can create a critical mass of people who think and behave differently has led to their use for that purpose. Because leaders are such important role models for the behavior of all other employees, changing the thinking and behavior of senior leaders almost automatically cascades down through the lower levels of the organization.

Examples of the use of learning to change companies' culture and mindset include the Prudential Insurance Company example of a new corporate strategy (for a detailed account, see Chapter 8; AlliedSignal's use of training in total quality to change the entire organization's mindset; *USA Today's* use of learning to help leaders trained as "poets" to think more like businesspeople; and SBC Communications' use of learning to forge together a new company culture from its disparate elements.

University-based Concentrated Learning Programs

Shorter periods of concentrated learning are becoming the rule in American corporations. Gone are the days when companies could afford to have their leaders off the job for periods of two, four, six weeks or even longer for "training." Today about the longest learning period American corporations can tolerate is one week. The popularity of shorter sessions, from a half day to three or four days, is rapidly increasing. Companies have found that the combination of shorter learning sessions, with the opportunity for learners to immediately apply what they are learning to their jobs and their lives, is more effective than longer concentrated learning sessions. The iterative process of learning, doing, learning, doing has also proven a very effective adult learning methodology.

Related to the shorter period of concentrated learning is the decreased use of university learning programs. The premier leadership learning programs, those at Harvard, Stanford, Wharton, Northwestern, the University of Michigan and other top schools, are finding it more difficult to recruit American participants for their longer development programs. The longest of these, like the eleven-week programs at Harvard, are simply too long for most American executives to be off the job. As a result, all the premier schools are now offering abbreviated programs that pack as much learning as possible into shorter time periods.

Another reason for the decreased popularity of university programs is that most are based on one participant per company, so the offerings must be broad in their curriculum design to apply to all participants. Today what companies need are learning programs that several if not many of their employees can participate in at the same time, with curriculum specifically designed to fit their present learning needs.

Some universities now design and deliver learning programs to fit the specifications of individual corporations. In these programs only employees of that corporation participate, so they are learning together the same things at the same time from the same teachers and experts. This is all good for effective learning. The drawback of university-delivered corporate programs is that most universities that offer these products are constrained to using only their own faculty. No university has faculty of universally world-class quality in all subject areas; so some subjects are taught better than others.

The best alternative for organizations needing focused learning is to combine several of the elements above. After an organization assesses its specific learning needs, a curriculum is designed to directly meet these needs in the most efficient way. Faculty—teachers and experts—are "cherry-picked" from the best available anywhere in the world and built into the learning process. The organization then manages delivery of the learning to make it the most time-effective and cost-effective possible.

University-based Learning Consortia

Another option for organizations that need learning but have limited budget resources is participation in a learning consortium. A learning consortium is formed when several organizations with similar learning needs band together. Essentially they pool their limited resources to make the learning they need for their employees available at lower financial cost.

In this arrangement, a curriculum is designed that responds to the shared learning needs of all consortium members. It is staffed with the best faculty available, and the learning program is delivered to participants from all consortium member companies at the same time. The consortium approach allows its members to access top-quality learning at a cost significantly less than would be required to have its own exclusive program of the same quality. The costs of design, faculty and delivery logistics are all shared.

The consortium approach also allows each member company of the consortium to send groups, or teams, of their employees to learning sessions at the same time. Team learning is more effective at building a critical mass of people with new ideas, who think and behave differently, than is individual exposure to learning (such as occurs in most university programs). The use of learning consortia has been steadily increasing in recent years.

Learning consortia may be free-standing, or may be university-based. One of the oldest and most effective learning consortia is the Thunderbird International Consortium (TIC). Formed in 1991, its purpose is to provide American business professionals with a quick and intensive introduction to doing business outside the United States. The host school, known officially as The American Graduate School of International Management and informally as Thunderbird, was almost a perfect venue to build such a program. It has an international faculty of top teachers from all over the world; its student body includes representatives of perhaps forty countries at any given time, making its Phoenix, Arizona campus a microcosm of world business; and the quality of the education it delivers is second to none. (Thunderbird was ranked by both *The Wall Street Journal* and *U.S. News and World Report* as the number one provider of graduate programs in global business education in 2001.)

The Thunderbird International Consortium consisted of eight companies when it was formed in 1991. All found themselves with the need to better prepare their managers and executives for doing business outside the U.S. None was able, on its own, to afford the cost of a customized learning program. But by banding together in the Consortium they were able to build a two-week learning experience that fulfilled their learning needs at an affordable cost. Each class consisted of a team of five to eight representatives of each member company; normal total class size was between forty and forty-eight participants. None of the member companies was a direct competitor of any other member company.

The curriculum consisted of the most important topics for preparing U.S.-based business professionals to successfully operate outside the U.S. They included both "hard" topics, like finance and marketing, and "soft" topics like culture and business environment. Each two-week session included a visit to a business location outside the U.S.

The combination of topical relevance, team learning, top-notch faculty and continually-updated curriculum design has made TIC so successful that there are now four TICs meeting at Thunderbird each calendar year, with a total of over thirty companies participating. The need for learning about international business accelerated steadily throughout the 1990s, and the TIC has continued as a leading source of that learning today.

Consulting Firm Consortia

Another example of a highly effective consortium, this one freestanding, is Global Consulting Alliance's Human Resource Learning Partnership (HRLP). Global Consulting Alliance (GCA) is a small, tightly-focused firm that consults to organizations on managing their human resources. Thought leaders in the field of HR, the principals of GCA wanted a vehicle by which the entire profession of human resource management could be advanced. Learning programs were available at universities, but all had significant limitations on learning, such as class size, the inability to send company teams and inconsistent faculty quality. Thus, the first HR Learning Partnership was formed in 1997.

The first HRLP consisted of nine companies, all non-competitors with each other, that came together committed to sending five of their best senior human resource professionals to a two-week learning experience in each of the next three years. Each year five different professionals would participate, so that by the end of the three years each company would have sent fifteen of their best and most promising HR professionals to the learning experience. The fifteen form a critical mass of forward-thinking HR leaders in their company; and together the total by 2001 of over 250 program participants form a critical mass for moving forward the entire HR profession.

Taught by the best HR educators in the world, the HRLP provides a base for research, practice and network building for the future leaders of the HR profession. Unlike some consortia that are formed for the express purpose of reducing learning costs, the HRLP's purpose is to make learning available that is unavailable anywhere else. It has proven so successful that now two HRLPs are operating, with fourteen companies participating; and plans are underway to form an HRLP in Europe.

Combined Program Learning

Another trend in executive and leader development is to use a combination, or "cocktail," of different tools to more quickly and effectively develop leaders. The ingredients in this cocktail include **360° feedback, focused individual evaluation of high-potential leaders, executive coaching, learning tied more closely to succession planning** and **learning as a continuous process.**

Since becoming more developed in the 1980s by firms like PDI and the Center for Creative Leadership, **360° feedback** has become a staple ingredient in overall approaches to leader development. Leaders get anonymous feedback on their behavior from their boss, peers and subordinates; and compare the feedback to their own perceptions of their behavior. Discrepancies often occur between the reports of the various observers of behavior, which provide opportunities to focus on and improve the effectiveness of leaders' behavior.

When taken in the aggregate, 360° leadership behavior data for a whole company or organization provide a basis for prescribing learning opportunities for leaders. When widely-shared learning needs are identified, economical approaches to providing the identified learning can be employed. Most 360° instruments allow for aggregating and cutting the feedback data in many ways to allow examination of leadership patterns across an entire organization, or by sub-parts of the organization.

Most companies use 360° data only for leader development, the purpose for which the technology was designed. We are, however, beginning to see the use of 360° performance data for evaluation purposes as well, often with a tie to compensation. It is too early to know how this use of 360° data will fare. Our suspicion is that if givers of feedback know their data will be used for evaluation, and if those givers of feedback are also subject to the same use of data about themselves, they will "game" the system so that almost no one ever gets feedback that could diminish their performance evaluation. This will, of course, result in the 360° feedback being much less useful for developmental purposes.

Focused individual evaluation of high-potential leaders was introduced at forward looking companies like General Electric several decades ago, and has found increasing use over the past several years. Typically, only a few (twenty or less in a large company) leaders are evaluated in a given year. These in-depth evaluations may be conducted by internal evaluation professionals, or by external experts. They often take up to three days of intensive testing and interviews, of both the executive being evaluated and of others.

Data are collected about the executive being evaluated and are used to coach the executive to help him or her improve their leadership performance. These in-depth evaluations are costly in both time and money, so are almost always used to improve leaders of already-proven competence. In the past, people selected for such evaluation often felt their performance was lacking and that they needed to somehow be "fixed." Today, however, individuals selected for intensive evaluation and coaching recognize it as the company's investment in them and their future, and welcome the opportunity for improvement.

The use of **executive coaching** has experienced explosive growth over the past several years. There are two primary reasons: (1) the relatively low unemployment rate in the U.S. has made it necessary for companies to develop leaders from within their existing ranks, rather than sourcing them from other companies; and (2) leaders must be developed as quickly as possible. Executive coaching expedites both these goals.

A "coaching network" now exists on the Internet through which organizations can identify and contact trained, competent executive coaches. The techniques these coaches employ can vary from interviewing, to instrumented data collection, to shadow coaching, to practice sessions, to instant critiques on just-completed behavior. While sometimes expensive, executive coaching can reduce the development time of leaders by a significant amount.

Leaders in the field of coaching, like Marshall Goldsmith of the Alliance For Strategic Leadership (A4SL) and Gary Ranker of Transinfo Inc., have perfected coaching techniques over the years and taught them to a rapidly-increasing number of professionals entering the profession. A caveat is important here, however: many unqualified people now purport to be executive coaches, and can do more harm than good in leaders' development. Before engaging the services of a coach, it is prudent to carefully check credentials and several references.

Executive **learning is now tied more closely to succession planning**, and **learning is looked at more as a continuous process**, rather than as merely a series of events. Succession planning, in its incipient form, typically began with a company's organizational chart. For each position on the chart, several possible replacements for the incumbent were identified and listed on the "succession plan." Often described as the plan for replacement if the incumbent "were hit by the proverbial beer truck," such charts were simply replacement plans, not true succession plans.

Thankfully, the art of succession planning has evolved since then. Good succession plans are now built around identification of the capabilities necessary for effectively leading an organization. People with potential to acquire the necessary knowledge and skills are also identified, and plans are laid for those people to acquire the identified knowledge and skills. A company's learning architecture is built to enable the learning of the requisite skills by the appropriate people.

For each person who needs to learn leadership information and capabilities, a development plan is crafted. The plan identifies specific learning needs, and the timing and source from which they will be satisfied. When taken in aggregate, the combined learning needs of everyone in the organization provide the basis for the learning architecture.

While certain learning needs may be specific to only one or a few people, many are common to large numbers of developing employees. It is more efficient for the organization to satisfy these common learning needs internally, on a large-scale basis. This is often done through learning processes for groups of employees such as leadership development programs.

For those learning needs that apply to only a few people, learning plans unique to just those people are set. They often involve those people attending learning programs outside the company, such as at a university; or self-paced interactive individual learning using computers or distance learning.

Today, the best succession plans provide for people with potential to craft a roadmap for acquiring the learning they need. They identify the required learning, where it will be acquired, how and when. The learning is a continuous process, so that the person is constantly learning something in pursuit of their long-term learning goals. No year in a person's career passes without significant learning.

Because up to 90% of someone's development results from on-job experience, the most careful attention is paid to the succession of jobs a developing leader has. The job progression is thoughtfully designed so that the person is constantly learning and broadening their knowledge and skills. With each new job comes the requirement for different learning, so the learning plan is constantly being revised and updated. The best companies pay constant attention to their developing employees' learning needs. As learning needs change, ways to acquire the needed learning are immediately made available.

A continuous approach to learning acts as an important aid to **retention of high-talent employees**. Today's labor market is such that any good person can easily find one or more attractive jobs outside their present employer. In effect, all good employees today are volunteers. So good employees need reasons to stay where they are. One of the best reasons any growth-oriented leader might have to stay with an employer is that the employer provides for their continuous learning and personal growth. As long as high-potential employees perceive they are constantly growing, they will be inclined to stay with an employer.

Another significant trend in corporate learning is that **learning is more strategic**. One of the most important components of an organization's competitive capability is alignment of the entire workforce behind the company's strategy. Through learning, companies are able to educate their workforce about their strategy and each employee's role in achieving the strategic goals. As a result, the focus of companies' learning has become more strategic. This is not to say that tactical learning has been displaced—it hasn't. It has merely been augmented by strategically-focused learning for a larger segment of the employee population.

There is also a greatly **increased focus on the results of learning**. Over the past decade we have tended to concentrate on the *competencies* required of leaders; but paid less attention to the *results* of their leadership. Today more attention is concentrated on leaders' measured results (see *Results-Based Leadership*, Ulrich, Zenger and Smallwood, Harvard Business School Press, 1999). As leaders' results are more carefully assessed, so too are the results of leadership learning being measured. Learning that does not result in improved performance, both for the organization and the individual, can no longer be afforded. So every learning effort, regardless of form, is now being subjected to strict tests of added value. The *consequences* of learning are now as important as the *purposes and processes* of learning. Methods for assessing the value of learning are discussed in Chapter 4.

Chief Learning Officers

The increased focus on corporate learning has resulted in the creation and proliferation of a new corporate position—Chief Learning Officer. As described earlier, the CLO is responsible for all aspects of learning for the company, both organizational and individual. Leading companies were the first to create the position, and many others are now following suit. Companies that currently have true CLOs include Goldman Sachs (Steve Kerr), Home Depot (Gary Jusela), ChevronTexaco (Barry Leskin) and Williams Company (William Clover).

Shortage of Leaders

Perhaps the most pervasive trend in American business today is that virtually all companies have a critical shortage of leaders. This is a manifestation of several contributing factors. First, there is a "hole" in the demographics of the American population. Because of varying birth rates over the past several decades, there is now a shortage of people in the age 25–45 cohort, a segment of the population that has traditionally provided many leaders.

Second, in the early 1990s many American companies went through significant downsizing. Many of the people "downsized out" would be part of today's leadership corps if they were still around.

Third, and related to the cost-reduction efforts of the downsizing, another area subject to major cost reduction was leadership training. So a whole generation of potential future leaders was denied the learning that would have helped to better prepare them for leadership today.

Fourth, today's diverse economy is providing an unheard-of universe of opportunities for proven leaders. Because of the overall dearth of leaders, companies are willing to offer enhanced jobs, bonuses and additional perks for leaders at other companies to switch jobs. Inter-company mobility has become the norm, rather than exception, so the best leaders are concentrated in the companies willing to do what is necessary to attract and retain them. This leaves all the rest of companies unable to fill their leadership positions to the level they would prefer.

Finally, the e-commerce economy has grown dramatically, and will continue to do so. As it grows it offers opportunities for leaders in traditional businesses to embark on new, often more exciting careers, as well as the possibility of becoming wealthy when an e-commerce startup company goes public. The siren song of e-commerce has proven irresistible to many leaders in traditional companies, and has exacerbated the shortage of leaders in traditional companies.

The combination of the above trends has served to make learning much more important in today's fast-paced competitive economy. Many new approaches to learning have been and continue to be born as a result. A purpose of this book is to explore these learning approaches and make them available to readers who might wish to adapt them to their own situations.

The next chapter discusses such an approach to leadership development. It describes an accelerated learning process for leaders, named by its creator "Formula One Leadership Development." It is designed to be applied in any kind of organization, of any size.

CHAPTER 4

Accelerated Learning and Leadership Development— The "Formula One" Approach

I n industry today there is plenty of capital, and no shortage of new ideas. Technological advances give companies new product ideas faster than they can be exploited. Technology can be developed inside, rented or bought. Companies have learned how to create strategies for success, yet many fail.

Leaders of people are most often the missing variable in today's success equation. With an unemployment rate in the United States hovering between 4.0% and 6.0% and a highly mobile workforce, it is often impossible for companies to find enough qualified workers to fill their needs. But the news gets even worse: **as scarce as skilled workers are, qualified leaders are even harder to find.**

You can assemble a group of highly talented workers to work on a project, but without a capable leader, the project will falter and not progress to its greatest potential—possibly failing altogether. In most companies the leader shortage is the single biggest impediment to improved business results.

The first impulse for companies with an insufficient pool of qualified leaders is to lure them away from another company. In the past this approach worked reasonably well, although it was expensive and caused distortions in pay equity within the company (to say nothing of internal resentment). Today, acquiring outside talent is no longer a viable long-term solution.

There simply are not enough experienced, qualified leaders to go around. Thus, many companies are asking, "How can we grow our supply of leaders fast enough to fill our leadership void?" Fortunately, new approaches to leadership development make it possible for companies to cultivate internal leaders quickly and effectively. However, a company has to be willing to commit the necessary resources. One such approach is an innovative strategy that develops strong, effective internal leaders—fast. It is called the Formula One approach to leadership development.

The Formula One Approach

Effective leaders not only produce results, they do it while motivating, coaching, supporting, rewarding and developing those they lead. **The best way to develop effective leaders quickly is by combining real business challenges with just-in-time learning and coaching.** It is time-intensive and resource-expensive, but it generates results quickly. Here's how the Formula One approach works (see Figure 1.)

Figure 1:   Leadership Development Tools Used in the Formula One Approach

- Development needs assessment
- The company's performance management process
- 360° feedback
- High-potential identification
- Active learning challenge projects with success metrics
- Just-in-time learning
- Coaching
- Instruction by external and internal experts
- Communication and presentation skill building
- Stand-back real time learning: learning how we learn

Employees with the potential to develop into more capable leaders are identified through a performance evaluation process. This process focuses on both business results the leader has achieved and the behaviors used to attain them. Once identified, the leaders-in-training work through the Formula One Process.

At General Electric, for example, leaders at every level have their performance evaluated twice a year—a review of their results and the behaviors used to achieve them. Those found to have generated good business results but who have not fully supported the development of their subordinates are subject to increased scrutiny and developmental actions. Leaders who do not improve their leadership behavior are not advanced in the organization.

The most effective way for developing leaders to get feedback about their leadership behavior is through a 360° (multi-source) assessment process. This involves asking five to twelve co-workers to provide anonymous data about their leadership by answering a survey. Survey respondents may be their boss, peers and subordinates; and sometimes outside colleagues including collaborators, suppliers and customers. Summarized survey results provide a baseline from which participants assess their growth as leaders.

After the 360° feedback process, participants are assigned a **business challenge**. It must be a **real business issue**, timely and preferably urgent—one that important people are scrutinizing. The business issue has to be large enough to matter but small enough to manage, and relevant to the success of the larger enterprise in which it is embedded. The success of the challenge itself must be measurable.

At *USA Today*, teams of leaders seeking to improve their leadership skills were assigned business challenges designed to improve the strategy and operations of the newspaper. The challenges included: (1) creating processes to improve networking across internal departments; (2) increasing the speed at which the paper was produced; and (3) redesigning pages and features of the editorial content. The results contributed to *USA Today* now having the largest daily circulation in the United States.

Business challenges are assigned to individuals or small teams of not more than seven people. (Larger teams give people places to hide, which limits their learning.) The challenge should be time-bound—typically no more than ninety days.

The leadership learning process uses iterative cycles of learning. Working on the challenge project, coaching and evaluating progress is repeated as many times as necessary to produce both a successful business result and significant leadership skill development. A **coach** assigned to the project both assists and facilitates the learning of the participants.

First, the business challenge is described to the participant(s). Next, working with the coach, the participant(s) create a "game plan." Using the game plan, participant(s) and coach identify what the participant(s) needs to learn in order to succeed.

As the challenge project progresses, subject-matter experts provide participants with the learning material they require. This combination of just-in-time learning (learning what they need to know just as they realize they need to know it) and its immediate application maximizes the impact of the learning experience. Learning "locks" that are immediately applied are embedded into the participant's capability set.

Coaches, and Internal and External Experts

The coach is active throughout the process to provide guidance, direction and support. The coach initially knows more about the challenge and the skills necessary to master it than do the participants. Part of the coach's job is to spot the learning needs of the participants before they are needed, and arrange for their acquisition. Data from the participant(s) 360° feedback process provide guidance to the coach about areas in which the participant(s) can improve.

At a large Blue Cross Blue Shield organization, all leaders-in-training were provided with data on their leadership by a 360° feedback process. Participants then received personal, confidential guidance on how their leadership skills might be enhanced. Those who wished more assistance were supported by a trained coach who continued to guide their learning development, some for as long as two years.

The ideal coach has the following: (1) understands the company ("the business context"); (2) knows how adults learn; and (3) can source the expertise the participants need to acquire. The coach should also have some formal training in coaching skills and significant experience in their leadership development application. Qualified coaches may be found both inside and outside the participants' organization.

Coaches add value to the learning process in three important ways. First, because they are knowledgeable about the organization, they recognize the nature and level of expectations set by the organization's senior leaders. Second, they know how to "navigate" the organization to get needed resources and support for the challenge project. Third, they can anticipate potholes the project might encounter, and can acquire the types of learning the participants need.

At AlliedSignal (now Honeywell International), business demands threatened to cut short the learning experiences of several leaders. Through the intercession of the coach, the CEO (who was totally committed to his leaders' learning) made the call to continue the learning process despite the temporary urgency of several business "crises." (Such crises seem to occur often in the daily lives of businesses.) Intercessions by committed coaches are often necessary to prevent discontinuities in leadership learning.

A coach must have the knowledge and competence that will provide the most assistance possible to the participants. They must understand the dynamics of the organization and know the most important players. They must also know what leadership behaviors are acceptable and unacceptable. They are *guides* that facilitate the learning process in the most direct, efficient ways.

Coaches may be senior leaders in the participants' own company who have effective, proven coaching skills. Alternatively, they may be leaders from other organizations who are familiar with the participants' company or business. They may also be consultants or academics who possess the same knowledge and capabilities and have extensive experience at coaching emerging leaders. The coach's ability and commitment will in large part determine the success of the leadership learning experience.

Topical learning may also come from sources internal or external to the organization. Some of the best teachers are often more senior leaders in the same company. They not only have subject knowledge and leadership skills but also a comprehensive understanding of the organization.

Senior leaders at Ford Motor Company have taught leaders at the next level down, and those leaders taught the next level, and so on until learning about company strategy, goals and processes had reached everyone in the company. In the process, leaders at all levels significantly enhanced their leadership skills and helped to create a leadership "brand," which distinguishes leadership at Ford.

Senior leaders at the Prudential Insurance Company formed the core of expertise and information to literally "teach" the entire organization about its new strategy. Leaders teaching in pairs worked with groups of employees as large as 300 at a time to quickly create a critical mass of people who understood the new strategy and their roles in its implementation. Out of this effort came a group of 100 leaders with newly-developed skills.

As with all teaching, internal executives who "teach" in the learning process often learn as much as the leaders-in-training. Teaching others about leadership requires them to think clearly about their own successful (and unsuccessful) leadership skills and styles. As they identify and explain their leadership practices, they become more thoughtful, effective leaders themselves.

External experts provide learning in areas that are directly relevant to the project. If there is a financial or marketing component, experts in those fields come in to teach. These experts typically teach in one-half or one-day learning sessions.

Senior executives at SBC Communications learned about finance, marketing, globalization, customer focus and other topics with the help of world-class experts. Leaders at Bank One explored learning topics relevant to their bank's turnaround, again with world-class thinkers. At Amoco (now BPAmoco), teaching was focused tightly on the learning urgently needed by the company's leaders. In each case, the quality of the teaching provided by the external experts was critical to the value added by the learning.

So follows a caveat: companies that select external "experts" based simply on geographical proximity, lower cost or personal relationships do not receive top-quality information providers or cost-effective use of their time, resources and allocated funds. The results in terms of the leaders being developed are significantly less than when world-class experts are utilized.

Choosing qualified external experts is crucial to the success of the Formula One Process. Experts must be competent in not only their own specialty area, but also must understand the business context in which they are providing learning. Preparing external experts to teach requires internal liaisons that know what the experts need to learn, as well as the participants.

External experts may be academics, consultants or business practitioners from another company or business sector. Whatever the source, it is critical that there be a good match between the level of learning they must impart and their personal capability. Under-qualified external "experts," who may be less expensive but also less competent, will render the leadership learning process much less effective for the participants—and represent a false economy when costing the process.

The Iterative Process of Learning

During the leadership learning, the participant is able to step back from the process with the help of the coach to observe how learning is taking place. People have different learning styles, and knowing the most effective way someone learns is an invaluable tool that can be used throughout life. The iterative process provides a chance to evaluate several different learning styles. In effect, *leaders are learning how they learn.*

By compressing the learning process into less than ninety days, leadership development is accelerated. The Formula One Process allows individuals to learn in three months what they might require three or more years to accomplish at normal business speed. Speed is often the deciding factor in winning or losing a business competition. Thus, it is vitally important that an experienced content expert provides cutting-edge learning in order for the company to apply the new practices as soon as possible.

Pulling It All Together

The Formula One approach requires a good deal of orchestration. The "Orchestrator" choreographs the entire production. This internal person may be the Chief Learning Officer or the Chief Knowledge Officer, the head of management and leadership development, or the head of training.

The job of the Orchestrator is to conceive the learning plan, help with selection of the participants, assure that the challenge projects are meaningful and meet the criteria for the Formula One Process, and manage the entire learning process. This person also oversees the choice of coaches, sources the learning subject experts, and prepares both the coaches and the experts for their roles.

An important task of the Orchestrator is to represent the process and its participants in all interactions with top management. Enthusiasm for the process can wane if senior management is not continuously updated on the participants' activities and progress.

At Honeywell International (formerly AlliedSignal), the Orchestrator role was filled by the company's Chief Learning Officer. He constantly apprised senior management of the leadership development efforts. When special leadership learning was required, he created the learning vehicles and helped identify the participants. When it became necessary for leaders to learn how to better negotiate deals with Chinese partners, the Orchestrator implemented the required learning and had it in use within only ninety days. One of the Orchestrator's roles is to ensure that learning is available "just-in-time" when it becomes needed.

Finally, the Orchestrator may be a buffer between the leadership learning process and pressures that could stifle or minimize it. Requirements of the participants' regular jobs, time pressures from day-to-day responsibilities and deadlines, and unforeseen emergencies can all conspire to delay or even derail the Formula One Process. It is the Orchestrator's task to keep all these pressures at bay until the participants complete the cycle of leadership learning. Steps in the Formula One Process are outlined in Figure 2.

Potential Gains for Participants

Emerging leaders who go through the Formula One Process never truly "complete" the process. One outcome of learning how they learn is that the leaders continue to learn more quickly throughout their careers. Another outcome is that they acquire coaching skills that make them better developers of subordinates and other

Figure 2:   Steps in the Formula One Process

1. Assess what the participants need to learn
2. Identify candidates for development, using the performance management process
3. Conduct 360° feedback surveys
4. Identify action/challenge projects
5. Match candidates with projects
6. Identify and assign coaches
7. Identify specific learning needed
8. Identify and select providers of needed learning
9. Create "project plans" for leadership development process
10. Orchestrator and coaches manage entire game plan
11. All involved review outcomes of the development process and lock in the learning

colleagues. Once kick-started, their development as effective leaders continues at a rapid pace.

The business challenge project gives participants new business knowledge and skills. Often it provides them with a window onto parts of business with which they had no familiarity before. Many get excited about new business areas and change their career paths. At Blue Cross, an executive in human resources became so excited about a corporate strategy project that she made a full career shift into the organization's strategy group.

Challenge projects do not all fit neatly into sixty or ninety day timeframes—some continue well beyond the learning and coaching period. In addition, participants occasionally continue with the project, sometimes even leaving their old job to do the project full time. As a result of their involvement with a project in its early stages, they may be the best person qualified to prosecute or even lead it. Figure 3 lists some of the gains that accrue to participants in the Formula One Process.

Figure 3: What Participants Gain from the Formula One Process

- Confirmation that they have leadership development potential
- Valuable feedback from the 360° assessment process
- Ego satisfaction and self-confidence from confronting and surmounting a difficult business challenge
- Learning about topics relevant to their challenge, business and career
- One-on-one coaching about their problem-solving and leadership skills
- Opportunity to learn coaching skills
- Valuable feedback on how they accomplished their challenge project
- Increased visibility to "those who matter" to their career
- A time-compressed quantum step up in their business and leadership capabilities

Competitive Advantage for Early Adopters of Formula One

Leading companies, recognizing their urgent need for more leaders, are adopting parts or all of the Formula One Process. While expensive in terms of both money and time, it produces more effective leaders more quickly than any methods used in the past. As in the case of *USA Today*, business results often show dramatic improvement as a result of an organization's increased leadership capability. The advantages to an organization of the Formula One approach are found in Figure 4.

The business turnaround currently underway at Bank One provides another example of the value leadership development can bring to a company. Following the direction of its new CEO, the Bank began conducting an intensive development program in Summer 2000. In past months, the value of the company's stock has risen steadily, as Wall Street's confidence in the Bank's leadership has increased.

Figure 4:   What an Organization Gains from the Formula One Process

- Reinforcement and refinement of its performance management process to identify leadership development candidates
- Focus on its most promising present and future leaders
- Narrowing its investment in leadership development
- Identifying and prioritizing its most critical business issues
- Skill enhancement of senior leaders who become teachers and coaches
- Expanded pool of high-potential, rapidly developing leaders is created—"bench strength"
- Tough business challenges are addressed and solved by participants
- A pool of experienced teachers and coaches is created for use in future leadership development efforts
- A stronger leadership team is forged among participants
- Retention of key leaders is enhanced

While the value of an organization's leadership capability is an intangible on the balance sheet, it has real currency value with financial analysts and investors.

In order for participants to learn leadership skills most effectively, they must commit time to the process—typically at least a quarter of their working time but possibly as much as full time. In a business already running at warp speed, the time commitment can create a real pinch; it can strain the day-to-day operations of a business.

Nevertheless, for companies starving for more capable leaders, the tradeoffs of time, money and absence from "regular" work may be worth the sacrifice. Organizations need to know that the leadership shortage will get progressively worse for at least the next five years, as our moving global demographics exacerbate the situation. (Global population growth and unemployment are projected to decrease into 2010, as the median age of the U.S. population steadily increases.) The alternative to developing a company's own leaders may simply be diminished business capacity and results, or an inability to compete altogether. What company can afford these consequences in today's hyper-competitive marketplace?

As this book is written, we are seeing an increasing number of companies adopting the Formula One Process for accelerated leadership development, in whole or in part. We expect this trend to continue.

In the next chapter, we begin to look at innovative learning architectures and approaches to learning and leadership development. Chapter 5 describes the Equiva story. A new Chief Learning Officer, Dr. Gary Jusela, was hired to help merge the three disparate cultures of three different recently combined companies. Chapter 5 describes the inventive approach he followed and the success it achieved.

Innovative Learning Architecture: The Equiva Story

S tart with an ownership structure that included three of the most significant players in the industry, an organizational de-sign built around three discretely defined entities, each with its own CEO, a $42 billion annual revenue stream, 14,000 employ-ees spread out across the United States and absolutely no estab-lished internal infrastructure. This is the challenge that faced Equilon, Motiva and Equiva Services, the three companies that con-stituted the U.S.-based refining and marketing alliance of Royal Dutch Shell, Texaco and Saudi Aramco, at the beginning of 1998.

The organization was created with the expectation that through the combination of the Shell, Texaco and Saudi Aramco assets, signifi-cant synergies (cost reductions) would be realized through staff re-ductions and knowledge sharing and that, cut loose from the parent companies, the organization would have the freedom to innovate and reinvent the downstream oil business. In addition, throughout much of the country during the early going of this alliance, returns on refined products and marketing margins at the pump were the lowest the industry had seen in decades. What follows is **the story of the building of a learning architecture** within the chaotic con-text of a $42 billion per year start-up company.

Learning Traditions

Reaching outside of the heritage companies making up the new alliance, the three CEOs decided to bring in external talent to staff the lead positions in Learning, Human Resources, Diversity, Purchasing and Information Technology. The three parent companies all had significant histories with various learning, quality improvement and employee development activities. Royal Dutch Shell had perhaps the strongest tradition, having devoted considerable energy and resources to the strategic process known as scenario planning. It was Arie de Geus, former head of Strategic Planning for Royal Dutch Shell, who declared over a decade ago that the ability to learn faster than your competition is the only sustainable competitive advantage any company can enjoy. Within the U.S., Shell Oil Company was about five years into a significant organizational transformation process influenced heavily by both Peter Senge of MIT and Noel Tichy of the University of Michigan at the time the alliance was formed. Saudi Aramco had a long history of investment in employee and management education, as exemplified by its training and development staff of some 1,500 employees. Texaco also had made significant investments in leadership education and quality improvement in the previous decade. Given these histories, the three CEOs were of a common mind that the development of the alliance organizations would be well served by establishing the position of Chief Learning Officer (CLO) and an internal architecture to promote continuous learning. The three also resolved that they would go outside the parent organizations to staff this new role. This was done both to bring an outside perspective and to minimize the risk that one of the parent company's transformation processes would either dominate the new combined entity or be smothered by the white corpuscles of the other two legacy streams. Thus, an early and continuing advantage of occupying this new role as an industry and legacy company outsider was and is an assumption of neutrality with respect to the Shell, Texaco and Saudi Aramco learning traditions.

Catching a Wave

Day one for the CLO was nine months into the life of the alliance. There was no learning and development staff, no course catalogue, no learning offerings internal to the organization, and the leadership and employees of the organization were consumed with the pressures of establishing and growing a $42 billion enterprise. Learning was not the first priority on people's minds—survival ranked much higher. The CLO was faced with high winds, heavy seas and a lone surfboard. Within the heavy seas there existed a number of forces and activities germane to learning and development. Many consultants from a vast array of competing firms had been employed during the organizational design/transition phase of the start up. A number of those were still active within the system, assisting with various organization diagnoses, infrastructure development, strategic planning, and the design and facilitation of leadership retreats. Plans were in place and a team was dedicated to implementing an alliance-wide employee survey. The CEOs and other members of senior management were concerned about the welfare of employees through the organization transition and start-up process and were committed to using a variety of tools to check the organization's pulse. During the transition process, the senior leadership had developed a set of core values for the organization (see Figure 1).

Figure 1:   Core Values

Values and Respects All People: My actions are consistent with recognizing and maintaining the dignity of all with whom I interact.

Integrity: I seek to convey the truth, and encourage others to do so.

Customer Focus: I am driven to achieve and exceed customer needs by direct customer interactions, while using measurable feedback.

Excellence: I am focused on the pursuit of measurable superior performance, enabled through learning, goal setting and results.

Acting For The Greater Whole: My actions and decisions are based on the benefit to and impact on all of the alliance communities of which I am a member.

Plans were in the works to establish a 360° degree feedback process for all managers and employees, as well as an Employee Performance and Development Process aimed at reinforcing the values and building alignment around the alliance's performance goals. A 9/80 work schedule was in place for all employees up to and including the CEOs. This meant that people would complete at least eighty hours of work within nine working days and have a bonus day off every other Friday. There were, therefore, a number of elements in place suggesting that the leaders wanted to build an organization that would both perform at a high standard and would provide a high quality work environment for employees.

Three waves proved worthy of some good early rides. The first was the effort to develop the organization-wide employee survey. After an initial invitation to join the survey team, the CLO soon found himself responsible for the effort. A cross-functional multi-layer team (which included Delta Consulting) proved to be a fruitful instrument for shaping a comprehensive organization assessment instrument and an employee focus group process. The assessment provided a baseline of employee perceptions about the organization, demonstrated at least one vehicle by which management was committed to listen to employees' ideas and enabled the organization to coin the term "High Performance/High Values Organization" as a mantra for what they were seeking to create in the new alliance. The survey revealed that employees viewed the organization as (1) lacking a clear game plan to beat the competition, (2) missing out on significant opportunities for collaboration across organization boundaries and (3) insufficiently attentive to the employees' desires for career and financial growth. The learning from the survey provided clues about where to look as the search for other waves continued.

Lapses in living company values came along as a second wave to ride. The CEOs established an early habit of listening to employees in small group sessions. One of the prevalent themes from such conversations in the early fall of 1998 was that a substantial number of employees felt as though they were not being treated with respect, while others voiced the concern that, in many instances, management actions were not in the service of strengthening the alliance as a "greater whole." The CEOs declared these findings as major and asked for help in structuring values workshops where the senior team (roughly the top forty-five leaders) could establish better clarity on how the values should translate within day-to-day practice. Structuring and orchestrating these sessions provided an early and highly favorable exposure of the CLO to all of his senior leadership peers and provided a meaningful vehicle to directly support the CEOs' agenda.

Joe Jaworski and a small team of consultants from the Centre for Generative Leadership near Boston had been working with the alliance from the beginning of the transition phase. They had organized a number of leadership retreats and, at the time of the CLO's arrival, were highly engaged in a series of "deep listening interviews" with the senior team to build an early understanding of the emerging leadership culture and to identify the most fruitful areas for development. This initiative constituted the third wave. Teaming with the external consultants and the two chiefs of staff from Equilon and Motiva, the CLO helped to create an intervention that enabled the Alliance Leadership Team to both hear the data that emerged from those interviews and to organize themselves to act on the findings. The interviews revealed three prominent areas of concern: (1) there seemed to be no sense of a "true north" for the organization; that is, the strategic priorities and game plan were unclear; (2) there existed no clear model for leadership and decision making, especially for issues that crossed organizational boundaries; and (3) there was a perception that a few of the level two leaders enjoyed positions of great prominence and influence, while the majority felt they were left out in the cold, a finding characterized and labeled as "few 'ins' and many 'outs.'" Within the context of a leadership retreat, this feedback was provided and digested, and substantial steps were taken to pursue follow-on action. Teams were formed to address direction, governance, a leadership model and employee engagement. Out of this process emerged a significant improvement in clarity around these fundamental issues and a roll-out process to engage every employee in the alliance in an opportunity to both understand and build alignment around the emerging strategic direction. The CLO was invited to join a team of six senior leaders plus the three CEOs to help establish what would become the overall strategic business direction for the new enterprise.

The combination of these three waves provided two important benefits for the CLO. First, these occasions provided venues to make a meaningful contribution of both content and process to the development of this nascent organization. Second, through the intense interaction and high pressure/short timeframe nature of these events, they provided the opportunity to establish some of the working relationships, visibility, credibility and political support that would be necessary to establishing a sustainable learning architecture down the road.

An Architecture Emerges

Mid-November of 1998 provided an exciting occasion. After three months in place, the CLO was joined by his first official employee. This initial doubling of capacity was indeed a magnificent moment, one that instantly extended the reach and potential of the learning and development function. Over the next four months additional staff was brought on board out of the U. S. operations of Shell and Texaco and one person was added from outside the industry. The expectation of the CEOs was that staff organizations throughout the alliance be held at lean proportions. Learning and Development would be no exception. The organization became fully staffed with nine employees. What this meant was that every opportunity to provide professional services must be scrutinized carefully for the leverage it provided both in terms of the richness of its potential impact on organization performance and employee well-being (remember the mantra High Performance/High Values Organization) and the opportunity it afforded for extending the reach of the learning and development activity through broad dissemination, replicability or infrastructure deployment.

Deliver the goods as you evolve the architecture. This is survival skill number one for birthing a learning activity within a new high pressure/high demand organization. The actual need for learning and development services in a start-up context is quite high. Clients may not be lined up to ask for help, but they are ready partners when the right business-oriented and collaboratively-generated solutions are proffered. Offering the right help is a matter of careful listening and observation. The learning staff must be continuously engaged with the real people in the real places of work, not isolated off in a corporate tower in endless sessions of inwardly focused planning and development. Learning architecture is best conceived out of a dynamic engagement with all levels of employees and leaders. Within the alliance, six areas of focus emerged for Learning and Development out of this dynamic engagement with the enterprise:

- Consulting Services
- Core Curriculum Development and Delivery
- Organization Assessment/100 Best Companies to Work for Initiative
- Knowledge Management
- Executive Development Course
- World Class Human Resources Function

Consulting Services

Consulting Services was the first and most obvious early priority. Starting out with no staff there was virtually nothing else to offer. Moreover, applied to the right business problems, the provision of consulting services offered an ideal opportunity to gain some quick wins, build relationships and get a read on how best to intervene from a broader learning perspective. The opportunities to provide consulting exceeded the available resource, so discretion in choosing projects was critical, and also provided the opportunity to broker the use of capable external talent from Shell Oil or from outside firms, but to do so in a way that would build a coherence and integrity to the practice. Consulting interventions that have proved most fruitful have been those in support of senior leadership strategy development and team building, inter-organizational conflict resolution and partnering with Human Resources to assist in the creation of the critical elements of HR infrastructure.

Core Curriculum Development and Delivery

While no curriculum was in place at the time the CLO arrived, many courses were advertised from external sources, principally from the many divisions of the U. S.-based portion of Shell Oil Company. Demand for participation in conventional classroom training was very low throughout the start-up phase. There was simply too much work to be done for people to either seek out or have the time to attend classes. All of the parent companies had learning offerings available, but added together they did not create a united whole. Part of the architectural challenge for the alliance learning team was that of understanding the most urgent learning needs, sifting through the many available learning offerings, and then clarifying what should be adopted and what should be created as the preferred, focused and finite set of offerings and delivery vehicles. The peak time for classroom-based learning seemed to have passed. The crush of competition and the demand to do more with less was necessitating an integration of learning with practice through more customized action learning designs and bite-sized learning modules delivered either at the work site or electronically through the web.

Organization Assessment/100 Best Companies to Work for Initiative

Having ridden the early wave of the employee survey process, the learning team recognized that extra momentum for the survey process was generated when the team spotlighted the comparison results with those of the 100 best companies to work for as designated by *Fortune* magazine. In the instances where the survey questions closely matched those in the *Fortune* competition, there were substantial negative gaps in the responses relative to those of the contest winners. Seizing on this gap, several key members of the alliance leadership, including two of the CEOs, tasked the organization to make the changes necessary to permit a challenge for the 100 Best Companies recognition. This leadership enthusiasm boosted support for many of the priorities the team would seek to advance through the learning function, including building strategic alignment, engaging the full talents of the workforce and providing a work environment conducive to professional satisfaction, growth and organization capacity building.

Knowledge Management

Substantial synergies had been achieved through consolidation of many staff functions and the streamlining of operations. Other organization efficiencies, however, could only be realized through the effective capture and redeployment/transfer of successful practices across organizational boundaries. In the service of capturing more of these efficiencies and building on the $800 million of synergy savings already realized, the learning team established Knowledge Management (KM) and its associated disciplines and tools as a high leverage practice area across the organization. Many operating units had focal staff designated to foster practice exchanges across geographic and institutional boundaries. The Learning and Development team seized the initiative to create an Alliance-wide Knowledge Management Council to provide policy and practice guidance to the organization's KM initiatives. This area of practice was viewed as being of particularly high leverage given that, with a little guidance and early support in infrastructure development, most KM activities were self-organizing and would gain a life and momentum of their own. Already within the Technology Center and linking across all ten alliance refineries, staffs had formed thirty independent and self-managing TechNets, or technical networks, to foster effective knowledge and practice sharing and transfer around specific subjects relevant to the art and science of oil refining. Other practice-sharing efforts were gaining deep holds in the arenas of health, safety and environment disciplines and refinery reliability.

Yet, while KM plays a crucial role in the development of an enterprise, practice sharing and transfer is not sufficient to realize fully the broader expectations of organization reinvention.

Executive Development Course

A key priority emerging from the alliance direction-setting team was that of creating value, by which was meant that the organization needed to identify new ways of using, organizing, acquiring and/or divesting assets to foster new value creation for both customers and shareholders. With this in mind and recognizing the run and maintain mindset within which most alliance employees had grown up in their oil industry careers, the CLO determined to create an executive development intervention aimed at building entrepreneurial leadership skills and fostering the development of actual new business ventures through an action learning design. By February of 1999, the CEOs endorsed a go-forward plan for creating such an executive development course and by March a design team consisting of a cross-section of seven alliance executives, three members of the Learning and Development staff and three external consultants (Nancy Badore of River Lane Consulting and Joe Jaworski and Otto Scharmer of the Centre for Generative Leadership) was launched. Through monthly meetings over the ensuing four months, interlaced with in-depth data gathering with Silicon Valley entrepreneurs, venture capitalists, new economy business leaders, and thought leaders in the arena of human performance and creativity, the team developed a learning design called The Leadership Laboratory for Competing in the New Economy. The design was launched in February, 2000. Mimicking the new economy in many of its elements, the Leadership Laboratory leveraged the learning of twenty-five participants across all 14,000 employees through the innovative use of an internal website and through multiple face-to-face forums for sharing learnings. The new approach to executive learning effectively cannibalized the historic sequential batch mode model of executive classroom education and would likely be cannibalized itself after three or four rounds as the learning team and the larger organization invented new methods of knowledge and value creation germane to emerging needs.

The Leadership Laboratory began with a three-day Ground School to orient participants to elements of the new economy, form learning teams and prepare for two- to three-day learning journeys out to new economy companies. Learning journeys occurred in teams of five accompanied by a learning staff guide during a six-week interim period between the Ground School and a five-day Retreat in a wilderness setting.

In the Retreat, participants processed their learning from the field visits, worked on developing personal insights on the individual leadership requirements for entrepreneurial development within the new economy and organized themselves to begin creating viable proposals for new business ventures within or adjacent to the alliance. Next, the participants managed their own process of investigating a venture development space designated by senior alliance leadership and generated not more than two to three business plan proposals. For the first round, the designated space identified was that of managing hydrocarbon logistics. Six weeks after the Retreat, the participants reviewed the business plans they created with a Venture Committee consisting of the three CEOs, three key business unit leaders, whose domains incorporated the designated venture development space, and an outside venture capitalist. Those proposals passing muster would then be funded, staffed and launched as new alliance businesses, potentially providing opportunities for participants to see into fruition the ideas they generated.

Throughout the 100-day cycle of this Leadership Laboratory, participants themselves would be responsible for teaching what they were learning to others across the enterprise through developing content for the website dedicated to this experience, through employee forums dedicated to sharing the knowledge and through their daily interactions back on the job, since the design integrated learning with ongoing practice in the interim periods between scheduled events. In order to foster the larger agenda of building a learning organization, the Leadership Laboratory placed great emphasis on the concept of each leader developing his or her own teachable point of view and taking responsibility to teach others what he or she was learning.

World Class Human Resources Function

Human Resources owned many of the systems necessary to support and sustain the Learning and Development agenda. Such systems as 360° degree feedback, performance management and succession planning were coordinated through Human Resources. Having these and other HR functions work smoothly was clearly in the best interests of the Learning and Development team and a strategic partnership between Learning and HR was a natural and obvious link. A fundamental objective of the Learning team was that of enterprise development. By helping HR develop its core systems through provision of content expertise, process facilitation and user training design, the Learning team both forwarded the objective of enterprise development and helped to put in place embedded systems to provide performance feedback, manage conflict and identify individual development needs. The relationship between Learning and HR has proven to be highly symbiotic.

Core Learnings about Learning Design in the Midst of Organization Design and the E-Commerce Revolution

Building a learning architecture within a system that itself is just being built may be an ideal experience to preparing to survive in the economy of the future. The learning and strategy disciplines have been preaching adaptive resilience and learning as competitive advantage for more than a decade. In the new world order of e-commerce, old business models and institutions are being destroyed as quickly as new Internet dotcoms are springing up across the landscape. Just as the theorists of organization learning have stressed the necessity for systems to adapt to changing environments, so too must the learning function adapt in this shifting world of global electronically-mediated commerce.

In the past fifteen years, large-scale change practitioners have integrated the strategic planning function with real time alignment and deployment into the enterprise with highly inclusive and interactive social technologies. As action learning advocates have proclaimed for years, learning need not be an activity far removed from implementation. The recent convergence of large-scale social technologies, the application of new science/biological models to human systems, and the evolution of connectivity through the information technology revolution make this a special moment in the development of learning practice. The new thinking combined with the new tools provides the opportunity to create dynamic learning architectures to match the dynamic growth of new enterprises. Learning practitioners must themselves be constantly at the task of learning if they are to serve the rapid learners who today are creating the new world of business.

Yet, while the task may be daunting, the learning sciences have an essential role to play. Employees still need to build the skills needed to perform at the highest level. While knowledge is being generated in the rapidly evolving enterprises of the information age, this knowledge must still be captured and organized in a way that allows others to derive collateral benefits. The new models and methods encourage self-management and self-organization, yet even self-management requires infrastructure. *The task of the learning architect today is that of creating the minimally sufficient infrastructure that allows employees at all levels to pull what they need from the system to accomplish their personal and professional goals.* Some of the processes will be mediated electronically, other elements will occur through face-to-face forums where objectives can only be achieved through the high context transactions of direct human relationships. And, of course, if they are to create the right content and the appropriate delivery vehicles, learning practitioners must themselves be constantly in relationship with the inhabitants of the systems and communities they are serving.

The learning architecture of the Shell, Texaco and Saudi Aramco alliance is evolving as, ideally, it should continue to do indefinitely. A few lessons, however, are already apparent. First, there is no luxury in a start up or dynamic environment (and increasingly are not all business environments highly dynamic—even the funeral industry is rapidly changing, yes?) of indulging in long periods of planning without doing. Just as action learning seeks to integrate learning and doing, the learning function itself must execute while in the process of planning where it is going. Second, integrating the customer into the planning and doing is a must. Only by deeply understanding the customer and the situation can the learning practitioner come to know the right waves to catch. Involving the customer as a partner in both the planning and development of learning systems simultaneously builds in quality and ownership. Third, staff for a lean operation; staff that has a diversity of skills to facilitate the reach across disciplines (OD, web-based learning, human resources management systems, instructional design, etc.) and the richness (sophistication and depth) to deliver all the required services. Staffing should be driven by demand, but should err on the side of lean. Assume that doing more with less will stimulate creative solutions and, where necessary, supplement internal staff with the judicious use of external resources. Small staffs make for smaller targets at time of budget review while promoting a deeper engagement of the customer in the design, delivery and operation of the learning systems. Finally, understand the ways of the new economy. Learn the new rules. Understand how the twin concepts of richness and reach play in the world of learning. Understand how the new internet commerce models can be applied cost effectively to building learning delivery systems both within the enterprise and within the extended enterprise making up the organization's ecosystem.

This is assuredly a grand time for the business of learning. Intellectual capital is king and the ability to learn quickly has never been more important.

This chapter was contributed by Dr. Gary E. Jusela, who served as Chief Learning Officer at Equiva, which is comprised of Equilon Enterprises LLC, Motiva Enterprises LLC and Equiva Services LLC. As this book is published, he is Chief Learning Officer at Home Depot, Inc.

CHAPTER **6**

Changing a Culture:
The Amoco Story

T his chapter highlights the evolution of learning systems at Amoco and their eventual demise with the acquisition of Amoco by BP. The chapter discusses: (1) the strategic use of learning to help the corporate culture at Amoco adapt to internal and external change through their Renewal Series; (2) the consolidation and expansion of learning opportunities throughout the organization for all employees; (3) the integration of both learning and internal organizational consulting into a Shared Services Model; (4) the development of Amoco's Learning and Development (L&D) Framework; (5) the use of the L&D Framework to help guide learning; (6) the Renewal Series Model with its strengths and weaknesses; and (7) some lessons learned and observations regarding Amoco's approach that relate to both internal organizational issues and issues external to the group relating to their clients.

Writers on dilemmas and polarities say that to understand centralization one needs to both understand and experience decentralization (Johnson, 1992; Hampden-Turner and Trompenaars, 1993; and Trompenaars and Hampden-Turner, 1998). Because they are interdependent, one or the other can only be understood and defined in light of knowing the opposite experience. Likewise, at Amoco, after a period of centralized corporate-driven training and development (T&D), from about 1980–1985, Amoco moved into a period of decentralization where sectors and business units handled their own T&D from technical training through non-technical (soft-skills such as management training, team training, negotiations, etc.). The interesting issue that arises under a decentralization scenario is the gradual unevenness of L&D opportunities that are available for people in the various business units. That is, some business units and departments continually use the L&D function to nurture their organizations and employee development and others let the function languish either from disinterest or cost-cutting measures.

This state of unevenness is one of the reasons that organizations move toward centralization (or its opposite) all over again. Another reason for centralization (from decentralization) is perceived cost pressures where the efficiencies of centralization seem to suggest much greater cost efficiency. A third reason is the use of learning as a key tool as part of a major change process, which is typically a centralized, hierarchically driven affair (O'Toole, 1995; and Miles, 1997).

Learning to Help Create and Sustain Organizational Change

As the 1980s ended, the senior management team at Amoco reviewed the industry landscape and decided that too many things were changing too quickly for there not to be a centralized focus to deal with overall corporate concerns. Thus, four major events occurred that emphasize the organization's shift in L&D focus and organization. First, senior managers met to determine the people issues that would be critical to the future of Amoco. Second, the corporation's president Larry Fuller declared that corporate renewal was essential in order for the company to remain competitive. Third, a corporate learning officer, Warren Wilhelm, was hired who quickly developed a strategic learning series for the top 100 leaders of Amoco. The series spanned an eighteen-month period and covered major strategic and people issues facing the industry and the overall business environment. This led to a stated need on the part of the top leaders to deliver the messages and needs to all the 3,300–3,500 senior managers throughout Amoco. Fourth, the Amoco Management Learning Center (AMLC) was formed. The staff of the AMLC would deliver a corporate sponsored renewal program designed to provide the learning that would enhance the management capability within Amoco. This learning would instill the necessity for change and the relevant principles, beliefs and skills for continuous renewal at Amoco.

The birth of Amoco's centralized learning system began with the following declaration by President Larry Fuller in 1988: "To assure that we...engage in corporate renewal, we need to develop and reassess our mission, values, goals and strategies. We then must define this direction in clear language and communicate it to the organization with the intent of creating understanding and ownership." As such, the senior leadership approved creating a learning program to help bring about this continuous state of renewal. The mission of the AMLC was to determine, design, deliver, and evaluate programs and experiences for Amoco managers worldwide that would help them achieve the corporate strategic direction. To take a page from the General Electric management book, Amoco wanted to achieve the right results, the right way in a changing industry.

The AMLC developed a series of renewal programs—the Renewal Series—that would broadly be used to create:

1. **Shared Mindset**: Common conceptual models/vocabulary and the ability of each manager to explain Amoco's strategic direction efforts.
2. **Alignment**: AMLC curricula consistent with operating companies and corporate initiatives.
3. **Improved Results**: Impact the individual, team and organization.

The Amoco Management Learning Center and the Renewal Series

To accomplish the centralization of L&D activities, Amoco created the corporate management learning center (AMLC), which was independent of all the other training and development functions within the corporation. This did not mean that the various learning groups in each sector did not "work together." Rather, involvement was one of cooperation not organizational structure. However, the people who created the AMLC were so busy staffing up and preparing the design for the first program that there was little true integration of work with other T&D activities. During the first year, the general approach was to deliver an early pilot. This abbreviated session was presented to members of the in-house Human Resources Organization Development and Learning and Development community so that they would understand what was taking place that may affect their own L&D activities. Later there was much more integration with different L&D functions because of some structural changes to the organization that will be described later.

There was a sense of urgency to get the Renewal Series up and functioning quickly. The AMLC staff hiring was roughly complete at the end of July 1991. The AMLC staff moved into the new leased facility in August 1991 and ran the first pilot program in December 1991. The first "official" week-long program was conducted in February 1992. Primarily an internal faculty taught this program, and all subsequent programs. The general rule practice was to (a) conduct a needs assessment of participants and senior managers, (b) hire relevant consultants to help the internal faculty design the program and (c) work with the consultants as they taught the first two classes. Finally, the consultants would watch the faculty present the material for two sessions and provide a follow-up critique. The faculty would then teach the remaining sessions. This practice was followed approximately 80% of the time. This practice was followed for two reasons. First, it was generally too expensive to bring in consultants for all sessions. Second, we felt it important to both try and model the fact that these ideas could be learned and taught by Amoco people and the behaviors they represented could be modeled in the behavior of Learning Center staff toward them and toward each other.

Target Audience and Perennial Issues

The target audience for the Renewal Series was the top 3,300–3,500 managers/leaders within Amoco's population of approximately 45,000 employees worldwide. The general definition as to who was eligible to attend was primarily based on "grade" within the company. That is, if someone was a Grade 13 or higher (grade being primarily determined by a "Hay Point" System), then they were eligible and mandatorily assigned to attend. In general, this was the first time that anyone could remember that a corporate function wrote to Amoco managers/leaders and "told them" they were scheduled to attend a L&D activity on such a scale. There were long-standing debates over who was eligible to attend. One such debate involved including individuals even if they were "Grade 13 and above" since they were not managers. The general answer was yes but business units were given the option to substitute within their allocated quota.

It was soon discovered that the grading system of managers/leaders was not equivalent throughout the corporation. That is, there was a significant population of managers in some business units that clearly were in important manager/leader jobs (plant managers of small chemical plants in the United States, similar positions among foreign nationals outside the U.S.) who were not included on the original list (there was no "single" list of managers/leaders by grade level) but were below Grade 13. While the U.S. population was relatively complete, the international population of appropriate managers/leaders had to be culled from multiple systems and lists. The basic rule to the businesses units was simply to review the list and substitute people if needed, but the unit was responsible for telling people (generally U.S. individuals) why they were not attending the program. As a result, more people attended in the first couple of years than was anticipated.

Evolving Program Design

One of the initial problems was what renewal at Amoco entailed. In general, the working definition of renewal was: A continuous process of change, improvement, and transformation allowing Amoco to become and remain a company where:

- Mission, vision and values guide action (independent efforts had been in place since 1989 to create and communicate the mission, vision and values of Amoco to employees).

- It is strategically managed and competing successfully. (Efforts had been in place but the Renewal Series was a key effort to move the company from a "project" to a "strategically" managed organization.)

- There is a minimum of organizational bureaucracy (during the Renewal Series there were at least two major downsizings and a major restructuring, inadvertently at times and planful at others, the Renewal Series program dealt with them all).

- The full talent and energy of all employees is utilized.

- Everyone feels the need for urgency to improve.

- Appropriate risk taking at every level is the norm.

- Empowered employees feel a sense of personal accountability.

- Everyone has an understanding and desire to improve short- and long-term business results.

Using these broad and ever evolving guidelines (i.e., definitions changed, different areas received emphasis at different times), the Renewal Series was initiated in February 1992. Another complication of the renewal was that other internal agencies championed one part or another of the corporate renewal mission. For example, groups such as the strategy group would oversee the issues of becoming strategically managed; the consulting group was responsible for issues of developing and communicating the mission, vision and values; the quality/continuous improvement group dealt with issues of the Baldrige criteria to run the business; and various individual

T&D departments were emphasizing learning related to a given business's strategy without necessarily relating their work to the renewal process. Needless to say and in hindsight, this looked like a cacophony of activities to the many people impacted.

Figure 1 shows the activities taking place from 1989 through 1999. The AMLC was only one of the twenty-three concurrent initiatives. As such, the AMLC competed (e.g., the quality/continuous improvement/progress initiative) with many of the other initiatives for time, resources and money. While it is an arguable point as to whether this was too many initiatives, it is certainly not more than seen at many firms. For example, Hamel and Prahalad (1994) point out all the initiatives that took place at Komatsu over the years of their growth and change. It appears that the real question is not how many initiatives there were but whether they were linked where necessary and focused sufficiently to provide a cohesive and

Figure 1:   Amoco Corporate Initiatives
Circa 1992–1994

Creating Renewal at Amoco: A Host of Initiatives

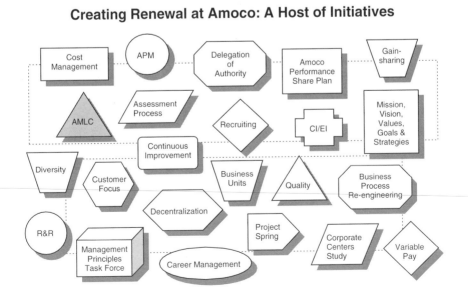

consistent picture regarding the overall strategy and change process taking place.

Table 1 shows the curriculum of the AMLC for the six years it was in existence. In reality, the AMLC Renewal Series represented the use of learning to create and sustain change in a complex business environment. Some would say the Series was highly successful and others would say it was not. The data show that it was well received, overall, and that many successful business practices resulted. Most importantly, because of the involvement of the senior executives as speakers and as participants, they were able to garner a sense of respect for themselves and an understanding of what they were trying to accomplish in a way that had not been done previously.

What is not shown in Table 1 is how the AMLC Renewal Series also took on the "hot topic" issues. That is, during the first part of the program, Amoco experienced its first major downsizing in approximately eight years. As a result, the Renewal Series became a focal point for discussions both of the material and of the rationale and purpose of the downsizing among the participants and with the faculty and senior Amoco executives. This had a positive impact. A significant proportion of the senior executives noted that they did not know how we would have gotten through the downsizing without the AMLC. The fact that participants talked to the internal Amoco faculty both in class and outside, allowed the AMLC to develop into the role of "sounding board" for the senior executives. This significant and critical role was handled with utmost respect. It was a policy that what was discussed by individuals at the AMLC was confidential and remained at the AMLC (i.e., what is said here, stays here). However, permission was given to bring up selected issues to senior management. At other times, comments that were heard frequently were simply aggregated and brought to the attention of senior management without attribution. This was known by the participants. (In hindsight, the role of sounding board could have been done more consistently rather than in the ragged and uneven manner it was handled.)

Table 1: Renewal Series Theme by Year and Topical Curriculum

Year	Theme & Curriculum

1992–1993 Program I	**Leading Renewal Through Our Strategic Direction**
	■ Design: Individuals from target group selected using a stratified random sample and assigned to a mixed business unit learning team for a week. Use of several senior executives throughout the week in "Executive Reflection" spots.
	■ Case study created on one of Amoco's business units used as discussion material.
	■ Topics:
	  ■ Why Renewal from the Chairman or Top Management Member.
	  ■ Leadership & 360° Feedback.
	  ■ Strategy: Corporate Strategic Direction and Model ala Michael Porter (Change at the Corporate Level).
	  ■ Continuous Improvement (change at the personal level).
	  ■ Integrating and Managing Change at a Personal Level.
	  ■ Personal Action Planning.

1993–1994 Program II	**Accelerating Renewal: Converting Strategies Into Action**
	■ Design: Individuals from target group selected using a stratified random sample and assigned to mixed business unit learning team for a week. Use of several senior executives throughout the week in "Executive Reflection" spots. Integrated computer-based business simulation designed after commodity industry.
	■ Topics:
	  ■ Executive Reflection on State of Strategic Direction.
	  ■ Teams and MBTI Feedback.
	  ■ Diversity Module (delivered by outside consultants)
	  ■ Computer Business Simulation.
	    ■ Team Work & Feedback Repeated Through Several Cycles.

Table 1:   Renewal Series Theme by Year and Topical
Curriculum (*Continued*)

Year	Theme & Curriculum
	■ Sharing Best Practices. ■ Leadership and the Skill of Managing Dilemmas. ■ Understanding Key Business Sector Dilemmas via Polarity Mgm't ■ Executive Reflection. ■ Action Planning.
1994–1995 Program III	**Continuous Success Requires Urgency, Courage and Action** ■ Design: See above. All is similar except that the computer simulation was changed dramatically approximately one-through the program and computer portion was deleted. The goal was to cause people to interact in such a way as to practice dialogue skills learned in class. ■ Topics: 　■ Understanding and Creating a Learning Organization (heavily influenced by work of Peter Senge & Chris Argyris). 　■ Pathways to Renewal (understand difference between problem solving and changing the system). 　■ Organizational Learning Concepts: 　　■ Left-hand Column, The Ladder of Inference, and Dialogue Skills to Balance Advocacy and Inquiry. 　■ Organizational Defensive Routines (based on work of Chris Argyris). 　■ Shaping a Capability: Amoco had added organizational capability assessment and shaping (i.e., developing needed capabilities) to their strategy process. 　■ LIFO Feedback (Instrument similar to MBTI providing feedback on interpersonal style.)

Table 1:   Renewal Series Theme by Year and Topical
Curriculum (*Continued*)

Year	Theme & Curriculum
1995–1996 Program IV	**Thinking Systemically: Learning Together to Drive Future Business Results** Design: Major change was that individuals came in teams selected by the business units with a "real" problem to work on. Definition of team membership was anyone who had a role in contributing to the solution of the problem. This meant that selection to the AMLC now fell in the hands of the HR functions of the businesses and corporate departments. ■ Key topics centered around systems thinking (derived from Peter Senge's work). ■ Creative Tension. ■ Views of Current Reality—Using Iceberg Metaphor. ■ Causal Loop Diagrams: Learn how to do these diagrams. ■ Outline team problems using this approach. ■ Learn Classic Stories/Archetypes of Systems as Templates or Schemata for many Underlying Problems. NOTE: Follow-up by independent observers showed that 61% of the teams made significant business progress on their problems/issues.
1996–1997	**Honoring the Past While Creating the Future** Design: Individuals in teams as selected by the business units with a "real" problem to work on. Definition of team membership was anyone who had a role in contributing to the solution of the problem. Selection of teams was the responsibility of HR group within business units. Problems were directed to be a strategic issue of importance to the group ■ Topics 　■ Understand Value Creation at Amoco. 　■ Know the Amoco Business Model (modified Baldrige model) and Understand Amoco Business Assessment Process.

Table 1:   Renewal Series Theme by Year and Topical
Curriculum (*Continued*)

Year	Theme & Curriculum
	■ Presentation on Organizational Learning, Organizational Lifecycle with Data Collected Based on William Bridges Model of Organizational Character which paralleled MBTI theory. Allow for direct comparisons. ■ Strategy Development, Deployment and Implementation at Amoco. ■ Understand Concepts of Accountability, Empowerment and Management Intervention at Amoco. ■ Understand and experience concepts that create "Elements of Structure" in organizations with particular attention to Amoco.
1998–1999	**Leadership for Renewal: Spirit, Purpose, Relationship and Action** Design: Participants in teams with a critical issue to resolve. The metaphor that the ideas presented would be new lenses with which to view the issues. This was the first year that outside consultants helped deliver a major portion of the material. ■ Topics: 　■ Understand the Competitive Landscape and How This Sets Leadership Context for Competitive Business Strategy. 　■ Understand Implications for Portfolio Management for the Corporation. 　■ Understand Critical Levers for Shaping a Culture Used by a Corporation's Leadership. 　■ Provide a Forum for Major Operating Businesses to Use the Lenses of the Program to Deal with Their Major Issues. NOTE: This was a major addition and design change. One full day of the program was devoted to operating business issues. This allowed the teams to cluster in their operating groups to deal with issues relevant to their own group.

Table 1: Renewal Series Theme by Year and Topical
Curriculum (*Continued*)

Year	Theme & Curriculum
	■ Merger/Acquisition: With the announcement of the acquisition by BP in August 1998, the program was altered slightly to deal with the issues relevant to the merger. In reality, the material was highly relevant to the merger. That perception varied depending on the perceived impact of the merger of the business units in attendance.

Note: The abbreviated topics listed under each program cannot do justice to the intricacies of design and the blend of head, heart and action that was consciously discussed and built into each module and considered for the total program in each year.

Consolidation and Expansion of Learning Opportunities

From 1992 until 1994, the Renewal Series operated as a major corporate-driven initiative within an array of other locally run T&D activities. In several cases, the T&D function within a business unit would deliberately try to align many of its major activities with the corporate initiative to insure some continuity and reinforcement of the effort that was directed at the top managers/leaders in the company. In other business units, the T&D unit would ignore what was going on in the Renewal Series but some of their subunits would pick-up what was happening and continue the activity. Therefore, you would find one refinery modifying the Renewal Series and delivering a parallel and reinforcing program to everyone in that refinery while the other refineries simply ignored the messages of the Renewal Series and delivered T&D based on their current and local set of needs. As such, some business units created what came to be called "mini-Renewal Series." These mini versions took key messages from the corporate Renewal Series and incorporated them with their local needs and ran independent but reinforcing programs. Therefore, the messages and learnings of the Renewal Series were unevenly distributed and reinforced throughout the organization.

Everyone in the L&D community recognized this incongruous situation and voluntarily participated in a L&D Council. They discussed what might be done to insure a more integrated and cohesive set of L&D activities while maintaining their own independence. During this period, the L&D Council suggested a new structure, which would integrate the L&D activities and direction of the corporation.

Independent of the L&D activities, the corporation was conducting a major study dealing with the concept of Shared Services. Under this concept, all common L&D functions would be consolidated into a centralized body offering "fee-for-service" programs. Thus, the perceived negative effects of centralization would be offset by the business demands of providing only the services desired by the business units. The fee-for-service reorganization looked like that shown in Figure 2. Pre-1994, the organization looked relatively traditional. In 1994, there was a major restructuring, which reduced corporate overhead units to minimal staffing and those that were required by

Figure 2:   Corporate Structure Pre & Post 1994

Amoco Organization
Restructuring - What's Changed

Shared Services Began in Late 1994

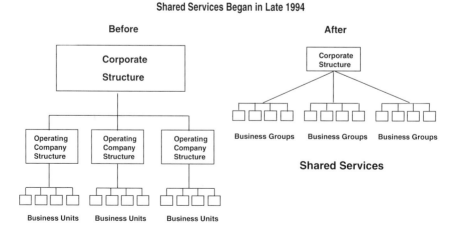

statute or absolute necessity to exist at the corporate level. Other "corporate type overhead" was placed in a Shared Services function and they were advised that they had to operate like a business or run the risk of being put out of business. As such, all of the non-technical training was consolidated into a Shared Services function.

Figure 2 shows a layer of functional services for the fee-for-service organization. This meant that the functions had to recover all of their "fully loaded" costs to include salary and benefits, overhead expenses, operating costs, etc. They were officially sanctioned to only recover enough in their charges to meet their yearly costs and to accomplish the financial goal of meeting their "net zero retained" expenses for any given year. The Shared Services function immediately put several major tasks on every Shared Services. The following list only highlights some of the issues that arose as this restructuring took shape. They were:

- How to organize your function as a Shared Services entity.
- How to understand your function as a business.
- How to calculate your fully-loaded costs.
- How to partner with the business units to determine the level of service that is needed.
- How to determine what staffing you should have to meet the services needed and demanded by the business units.
- How to deal with the pay inequities of people joining a consolidated organization from multiple businesses where pay is often very different. (Recognize that all costs had to be recovered by the Shared Services function. So, while you were moving to achieve pay equity you were trying to figure out how to sell enough of your services to attain solvency.)
- How to educate the business units about your services.
- How to determine the product and service mix that you would possess as an internal consulting unit in your discipline to the business units.
- How to market yourself to the business units.

■ How to determine which products and services should be kept inside versus outsourced (i.e., where do the businesses want to maintain "pairs of hands" versus a strategic capability).

Figure 3 shows several things. The most important here is that the L&D function was consolidated with newly created organizational capability group, which included both the OD Consulting Function and the L&D functions.[1] In general, this new Organization Capability Group (OCG) group was not the organization that the senior team doing the organizational redesign had in mind. However, the fact that the L&D community had created a document ready to present on a consolidated restructuring allowed the community to shape the new structure within the Shared Services concept. Once

Figure 3:   Learning and Development Embedded within the New "Organization Capability Group" Embedded within HR Shared Services Structure Embedded within HR Organization

Corporate Human Resources Organization

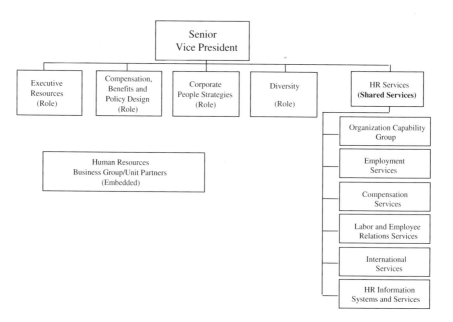

accepted, all individuals originally scattered throughout the L&D functions across the corporation were now evaluated for inclusion in the new OCG.[2] This chapter only deals with the L&D function as it changed and evolved in this process. In general, it does not deal at all with the organizational consulting side of the OCG and the developing and changing interaction and structure involving both sides of the group.

Figure 4 shows the composition and general roles of the OCG after several iterations. It also shows a parallel OD and L&D structure with Lead Consultants on the OD side partnered with Sector Learning Directors on the L&D side. In this way, the dual face of the OCG could be represented to the client regarding both OD and L&D issues to help achieve business results. The initial OCG organization did not start this way. While the OD side was generally organized in this manner, the primary organizational arrangement on the learning side was a series of "Learning Centers" (Tulsa, Chicago,

Figure 4:   Final Structure of the Organization Capability Group Prior to Acquisition by BP

Human Resources/Organization Capability Group

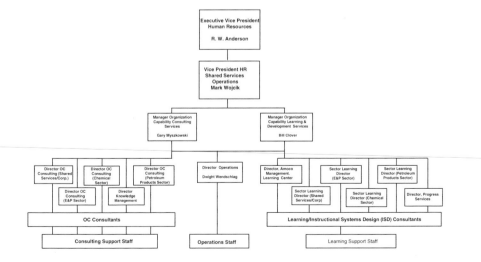

AMLC, Houston, and a "virtual" center in Atlanta). These centers delivered courseware on a regular basis to meet the needs of individuals and organizations in an effective manner using a few internal and many external vendors.

While the Learning Centers were highly successful and provided the continual revenue to all the OCG to operate in the "black" from the first year onward, there were other unintended consequences. This organizational difference was critical because it meant the focus of the senior learning person was what was delivered in the learning center and not necessarily what was needed in the business unit to achieve business goals. It resulted in disconnects in relationships, differences in power, differences in salary, etc., and turned out to be a pernicious internal problem to the OCG.

The major change to get to the structure of Figure 4 was to rethink the L&D side of the OCG around the concept of Learning Consultants and not the concept of Learning Centers. As consultant Linda Petchenik and others pointed out, the Learning Centers were geographically organized (e.g., Chicago, Tulsa, Atlanta, Houston) but the consulting side was organized as Account Representatives within the various businesses. It took two years for me to see the folly of the original organization before we moved to the one shown in Figure 4, which created a parallel structure to the consulting side of the OCG.[3] In the organization shown in Figure 4, the Learning Centers did not go away. Rather they continued to serve the needs of the OCG and the corporation as fee-for-service entities in the various geographic areas. They accomplished this by providing L&D programs that had a regular market and fell within the needs of the corporation. These changes freed the senior learning person to be a learning consultant and partner with the senior OD consultant in each business not a "geography" bound Learning Center Director. Learning Center Director positions were modified to give other individuals supervisory and management opportunities.

Most importantly, with the new organization in place it became important to create and establish a L&D Philosophy and Framework to guide the activities of the new organization in a Shared Services environment. A team of L&D colleagues created the Learning and Development Philosophy and Framework discussed below.[4] This Philosophy and Framework was approved in February 1995, just a few months after the restructuring into Shared Services. The L&D Philosophy was a simple set of statements regarding the organization's commitment to learning. The philosophy simply stated:

We believe learning and development at Amoco:

1. Is essential to developing the strategic and tactical capabilities required for business success.
2. Involves mutual accountabilities and responsibilities on the part of individuals, supervisors, and the organization and is consistent with Amoco's employment philosophy to grow individuals while we grow our business.
3. Must maintain a dynamic balance between the corporation, business groups and individual needs in a changing environment.
4. Is an investment with both short- and long-term returns and will be evaluated, assessed and held to appropriate standards.

The irony of these statements as with others that were approved by the corporation is that they belie the hours spent in focus groups and discussions before they were approved. Each one is, to use a trite phrase, "pregnant with meaning" and debate, etc.

More important than the L&D Philosophy, was the L&D Framework that focused learning into five key overlapping areas. The L&D Framework was defined to meet business needs through:

1. Development for strategic alignment.
2. Development essential for job preparation.
3. Development to grow leaders.

4. Development to maintain capabilities and to close capability gaps.
5. Development of basic competencies and skills.

It is essential to understand that the L&D Framework preceded the appropriate organizational structure by about two years. The appropriate organizational structure is shown in Figure 4 where there are senior learning consultants serving as L&D account representatives to the business units in the same way that the OD consultants were organized. In the new structure, the senior L&D consultants were partners with the senior OD consultants representing the OCG to the client business unit. Until that time, the L&D professionals were somewhat hamstrung by an organizational structure that focused on Learning Centers and courses taught in a geographical region as opposed to direct conversations with each business and its strategic and tactical issues for which learning solutions needed to be created. (The delay in creating these changes was the result of the author's lack of insight and leadership and belongs to no one else.) However, on the positive side, the Learning Centers were able to meet the goal of "net zero retained" from the very beginning and actually generated a "profit" every year. It turned out that this additional cash over and above expenses was critical for the OCG to manage the group by paying for development activities, major meetings, awards and recognition, bonus money, etc. So, while the Learning Centers retained their roles—providing fee-for-service courses on a market driven basis—the role of the senior learning person in each business sector was changed to be that of a partner with the OD consultant in helping businesses use OD and L&D solutions to deal with relevant issues.

L&D Framework Guides Learning

Figure 5 is a graphic depiction of the L&D Framework. The L&D Framework categories are arrayed across the top with the various employee levels down the left side. Within each cell under the categories are the exemplary programs. The box size gives you a sense

Figure 5: Amoco's Learning and Development Framework

Examples of Categories and Topics by Level

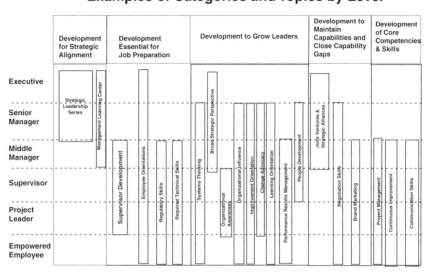

*Not meant to be representative of percentage of time spent on each category at Amoco overall.

of the appropriate target audience. Under the first category of development for strategic alignment are two major programs. The first was the AMLC Renewal Series that was targeted to Amoco's middle management managers/leaders and higher. Additionally, there is a category of programs called the Strategic Leadership Series that was targeted to the top 350 leaders at Amoco and provided as seminars on current topics and issues (e.g., Portfolio Management, Growth with Cost Control, Joint Ventures & Acquisitions, etc.). In general, programs that fell under the category of Development for Strategic Alignment were approved and directed to occur by the Strategic Planning Committee (i.e., Amoco's top executive management committee). This is important to note. These programs were "corporate driven." However, all other programs were generally major business units or lower business units driven all the way down to individual development plans. This meant that there was a fee-for-service philosophy instilled within the L&D Framework. The goal was to minimize what was corporate driven and to maximize the L&D

programs sought directly by the business units in their need to develop their organization or their people via their development plans.

Another important fact is buried in the Development Essential for Job Preparation column. The second category has a series of program titles such as team training, supervisory training, progress (continuous improvement/quality training) and technical training. While the OCG was not responsible for technical training, with the approval of the L&D Framework, this was the first public and formal statement that the senior management equated the importance of supervisory and other non-supervisory training with technical training. This public statement that non-technical training such as supervisory training, team training and training on continuous improvement was as important as technical training was a paradigm shift of the highest order in the thinking of senior management.

The Development to Grow Leaders category generally focused on individuals who had been selected by their business units as high potentials for special learning opportunities to progress them in their career. Note, in general, while there was an awareness of high potentials at the corporate level, their development, other than developmental assignments, was left in the hands of management at the business unit level. This process had both strengths and weaknesses that were becoming evident at the corporate level just prior to the merger/acquisition by BP. In this arena, the responsibility of the AMLC was to manage various consortia (e.g., University of Indiana, Thunderbird, etc.) and insure that business units provided the opportunity to attend these programs to various high potential individuals. Additionally, we created and managed an *Employee Resource Guide* that provided a list of schools and programs that the AMLC staff felt met the goal of providing learning geared to the various competencies in the AMLC competency model of leadership.[5] In the final year at Amoco, this resource guide was provided both in hard copy and online. Additionally, the online version had hot links to such services as Bricker's online so that HR managers could look for other programs they may need for individual high potential development.

The Development to Maintain Capabilities and Close Capability Gaps category was the area that came closest to organizational consulting for learning issues. Here there was a cadre of learning/ISD consultants whose responsibility was to work parallel with the consultants and help develop the learning materials necessary to help an organization meet its strategic needs. Originally, these consultants were embedded within the Learning Centers. In 1997, the learning side of the OCG was restructured to move the learning consultants out from under the Learning Centers and to create a parallel learning consulting organization. Therefore, the senior learning consultant in each part of the business (e.g., Shared Services/Corp., Chemicals, Petroleum Products, and Exploration and Production) worked in partnership with the senior OD consultant to provide the consulting and learning services necessary to meet the business's needs. This was an important organizational change. There were dozens and dozens of projects that were generated in this manner. One key example, as shown in Figure 6, dealt

Figure 6:   Learning Program to Help Chemicals Sector Facilitate Strategic Shift in Focus

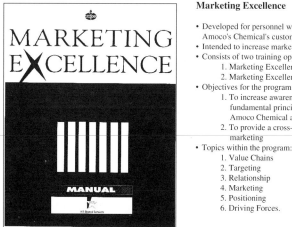

Marketing Excellence

- Developed for personnel who directly or indirectly support Amoco's Chemical's customers.
- Intended to increase market focus.
- Consists of two training opportunities:
  1. Marketing Excellence Overview (1 Day)
  2. Marketing Excellence Program (3 Days)
- Objectives for the program:
  1. To increase awareness and provide exposure to the fundamental principles of "Marketing Excellence" at Amoco Chemical and begin to apply them
  2. To provide a cross-sector common language for marketing
- Topics within the program:
  1. Value Chains
  2. Targeting
  3. Relationship
  4. Marketing
  5. Positioning
  6. Driving Forces.

with a change in focus and strategy in the Chemicals business. The focus was to change it from a commodity product business selling to a limited number of buyers to one with a marketing approach where there was a range of opportunities in the more than 100+ markets. Thus, a great deal of learning had to take place in order to understand the change in mindset, knowledge and skills that a "marketing approach" meant to the people within the Chemicals organization. After searching for a program outside to meet this need, it was determined that a customized in-house program, which combined external and internal resources, would work best. Given this, the Sector Learning Director in Chemicals oversaw the development and implementation of a major effort that involved learning about marketing and the model that Amoco would use. This effort resulted in a program designed to meet the needs of managers at three different levels of the Chemicals organization. In this way, the learning function helped the Chemicals business meet its strategic need to develop a marketing capability and approach to thinking about and selling their products.

The Development of Core Competencies and Basic Skills category represented the work of the Learning Centers. The Centers provided an array of over 100 courses that were market driven with over 90% of them being taught by external vendors at prices favorable to Amoco employees. In many ways, the Learning Centers became the "cash cow" of the organizational capability group. One key goal was to create "learningware" based on the strategic needs of the business units and then provide it through the Learning Centers in order to develop a revenue stream. In this way, the new courseware could be provided to the rest of the corporation and it would continue to be provided as long as the "market" supported it. In reality, the Learning Centers offered a variety of courses on every aspect of the Learning and Development Framework. Figure 7 shows the mix of courses offered in 1997.

The L&D Philosophy and the L&D Framework embedded within the changing corporate and OCG structure was the approach taken

Figure 7: Mix of Courses Provided Through the Learning
Centers in 1997

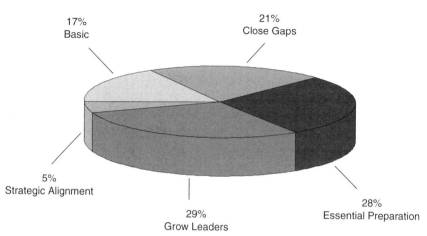

17%
Basic

21%
Close Gaps

5%
Strategic Alignment

29%
Grow Leaders

28%
Essential Preparation

to providing learning and development services. Given the dictum within the Shared Services Model for the organization to meet the financial goal of recovering all fully loaded costs (i.e., net zero retained), it was a success. It was a success within that objective but within the author's experience, that objective was an impure one.

The objective of meeting financial targets alone often drives the wrong kinds of behaviors. We saw this from the beginning in the OCG where consultants were driven to obtain any kind of work to meet billable hours as opposed to more impactful and strategic work that met the more impactful needs of the business units and the corporation. This was a key learning of trying to run an internal consulting and learning organization that was driven to meet "net zero retained." There were several built in dilemmas. First, all internal consultants (both OD and L&D) felt the need to meet billable hours. Second, clients often wanted to hire the consultants for immediate more short-term projects ("pair of hands"). This was the result of our clients needing immediate assistance, not seeing our consultants as the best resource for strategic work, and our clients not knowing what strategic work they needed. This led to continual internal tensions, which AMLC staff attempted to resolve by working with the senior managers, providing various L&D opportunities for the AMLC personnel, and trying to find the magic balance between short-term, billable work and long-term projects that were more important.

Overall, the L&D Philosophy and Framework were very valuable in guiding the thinking regarding what learning should be provided. They were also valuable in assessing what various business units and the organization were providing with regard to L&D. The L&D Framework can be compared to that of a five-room house where each room serves a key purpose and the goal is to furnish each room with the necessary programs to fulfill the needs of that room but constantly changing the "mix of furniture" within the room to keep it current and relevant. At the same time, viewing the whole house permits an assessment of where one area is too sparsely furnished and may be a source of problems in the future. An issue demonstrating this concept surfaced in the Development to Grow Leaders category. Over time, AMLC personnel recognized that this area really did not have the kind of structure and programs that targeted high potentials as a cohort group via group programs directed by the corporate office. The Renewal Series did get to this point. While several strong attempts were made, they were always rejected for one reason or another. Yet, just prior to the acquisition, there was a true felt need that the succession planning effort needed a revitalization that would produce a corporate-driven L&D effort to better insure the necessary development of the high potentials for leadership positions. Ironically, this is the one area where it was perceived that the BP learning systems excelled. Most of their L&D programs at the time only focused on the top 1,000+ managers in the corporation and the high potentials.

A key point to reiterate is that, with the exception of the Development for Strategic Alignment category that was driven by corporate direction at the Strategic Planning Committee level, all learning activities were market and business unit driven. All courses in the

Learning Center System had to have a buyer. As such, the learning system approach tried to use the market as an efficient way to determine what should be provided to Amoco employees.

Another way to look at the L&D Framework was that it allowed us to think about both Learning for Continuity and Learning for Change. Figure 8 provides a visual example of how the Framework could be used in that manner. Three of the categories in Figure 8 can be thought of as "development for continuity." These categories: Development to Build Basic Skills and Core Competencies, Development Essential for Job Preparation and Development to Grow Leaders are essential for the continuing functioning of an organization as it goes about its daily business. On the other hand, the three categories of Development to Grow Leaders, Development to Maintain Capabilities and Close Capability Gaps, and Development for Strategic Alignment are essential to meet the needs of development for change. The perpetual L&D challenges are: (1) understanding the various programs and experiences necessary in both categories; and (2) maintaining the dynamic balance that must exist between the issues of change and continuity. The L&D Philosophy

Figure 8: Learning and Development Framework as a Model for Different Types of Learning

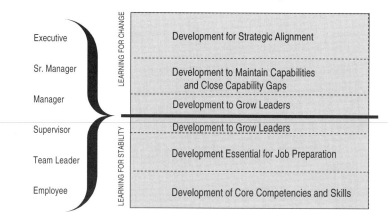

and Framework gave us a way to analyze and conceptualize the issues.

The Renewal Series Model: Its Strengths and Weaknesses

It is relevant to focus on the Renewal Series Model because it was a very visible attempt to transform Amoco at a time of perceived critically needed change. The Series was designed to help it become a learning organization by achieving the major goals of the renewal and thereby creating a culture that valued learning and change.

David Nadler (1995) notes that incremental change can be delegated but that the senior leadership of the organization must lead the transformational change. Charles Handy (1990) says that the first step in effective change is changing the language. There is sufficient data to suggest that the Renewal Series was relatively successful at instilling a common language and an effective set of models throughout Amoco that were used by many people throughout their business units.

Was Amoco a "Learning Organization?" Peter Senge (1990) is often quoted as saying that a "discipline" is a skill that is never fully attained but always continually practiced to gain ever higher levels

Table 2:   Customer Evaluations of the OCG as of August 1998

1998 Baseline Customer Feedback	Favorable (%)
How satisfied are you with the OCG services provided on this project?	94
Given a choice, I would continue to use OCG for the services they provided on this project.	94
I would recommend OCG to a colleague with similar business needs.	94
Overall value: How satisfied are you that the impact of the services provided by OCG are worth the costs?	90

of competency. Given that definition, Amoco was making strides toward becoming a learning organization. Yet, when BP acquired Amoco they systematically deleted every L&D program, organization and system that was put in place, although the Learning System had demonstrated that it recovered fully-loaded costs. Given this criterion, Amoco may have been a learning organization but it was not impressive enough to keep it from being taken over and downsized into history.

Closer Inspection

Let's first look at the results of the Renewal Series over the six years of its existence because it was the most visible example of the "learning" side of the business to the corporation. In general, the overall Series added value and the results were measurable and positive. This can be validated in several ways. First, the immediate outcome surveys dealing with the perceived value of the program were positive as shown in Figure 9. While these ratings only represent a Level 1 review in a Kirkpatrick model (1994), they are incredibly important because they are the starting point to insuring that people are

Figure 9:   Value Ratings of Six Renewal Series Programs

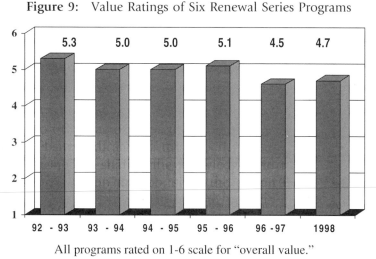

All programs rated on 1-6 scale for "overall value."

This 1998 program rating greatly affected by acquisition announcement.

willing to return or to recommend the program to others (another measure that was used from Year 2 forward). Recall from Table 1 that Level 4 analysis on the role of Program 4 did reveal business impact as well.

As shown in Figure 9, there was a gradual decline over the six years of the program. The first four programs were arguably the "best" in the view here. This does raise an interesting point regarding when you simply improve and modify a program and when you literally reengineer the learning approach. The drop in the final two years indicated the need to reengineer the overall approach and that is exactly what was happening when the acquisition by BP occurred.

There were two major efforts that occurred toward reengineering the Renewal Series. First, after the 1996–1997 program, Harold Hillman, Director of the Amoco Management Learning Center, led a comprehensive needs assessment regarding what should be included in the future programs. This led to a final Renewal Series program that was both centralized and decentralized—the first few days were devoted to issues related to corporate perceived needs and concerns and the last part of the program was developed by each major business (e.g., Exploration and Production, Petroleum Products, Chemicals, Shared Services). Ideally, each business would utilize what was being taught in the first few days to issues relevant to their own business. In actuality, some business units spent more time integrating the material from earlier in the week than others.

The second major reengineering effort came from the participants (the senior managers) and not from the learning community. Their basic assumption via informal feedback was that the Renewal Series had lost its impact, direction and relevance for the organization. This led to the Chairman's Council (most of Amoco's 75 senior executives) conducting an evaluation of the Renewal Series.

While we accepted, recognized and even welcomed the change because it would lead to opportunities that had not been accomplished in an effective manner (e.g., more targeted and focused programs rather than the generic Renewal Series program), I cannot say we would have done it without the "push" by the customer. Therefore, the learning community did not lead the change that occurred, the customers led the change. It is ironic that the reengineering effort led by the AMLC staff seemed to miss the desired changes of the senior management group regarding the nearly total refocusing of the approach and structure of the learning events known as the Renewal Series.

On the positive side, the senior executives suggested that the Renewal Series had accomplished a great deal as shown in Figure 10. These are formidable accomplishments. The following examples indicate the impact of these seemingly simple statements.

First, regarding the senior group's (Strategic Planning Committee, SPC) exposure to the organization. In an executive staff meeting of the Exploration and Production business, one of the executives remarked that he did not need to come to the Learning Center to hear

Figure 10: Strengths of the Renewal Series as Perceived by Senior Executives

- Instilled Common Mindset/Language (e.g., alignment)
- Fostered "One Company" Mindset, Reduced Silos, Fostered Sense of Belonging
- Energized Leadership
- Encouraged External Focus
- Provided Learning in Leadership/Management Tools
- Networking Opportunity
- SPC Exposure to Organization and Vice-Versa
- Shared Learnings
- Exposure to Corporate Performance Picture
- Team Focus (last two years)

a discussion of strategy. However, he was surprised to learn that very few of the people in the room seemed to know, understand or accept the strategic pronouncements he and his colleagues had worked so hard on. Thereafter, he readily conceded that a strategic learning session was extremely important.

The second example relates to the impact of the exposure of the senior group to the ideas of the program's participants. The participants related that they had developed a new-found respect for their executives as they listened to them discuss the decision criteria used to resolve issues that were paramount to the future of the organization. In general, the participants took away from the L&D programs a sense that their executives did take into account the factors they wanted them to consider even if they did not weight them the same way.

Third, during the early years, the CFO remarked that he had been riding the elevator with a group of participants after a plenary session to a breakout meeting. He had asked them about the "hurdle rate," cost of capital and other basic financial standards of the organization. He was surprised to learn that no one knew any of the answers. To this executive's credit, he admitted that this was probably his fault. The organization had not recognized the need for people to understand, or know, the financial picture, therefore, there had been no effort to inform the wider audience. (Recall that the audience for the Renewal Series was the top 3,300–3,500 people in the corporation.)

Fourth, the idea that the program fosters a one-company mindset became evident during a discussion involving seventy-five people on the issue of whether the Chairman had enough charisma to lead the renewal process. The debate was hot and heavy. After hearing the Chairman earlier in the day talk about the "why" and "what" of renewal, the audience was literally evenly divided over the "charismatic merits" of the Chairman. At this point, one of the participants raised his hand and stated, "I have been in this company 17 years. And, for the last 20 to 25 minutes, I have listened to a group of strangers debate whether the Chairman has the leadership abilities to change this company. In my experience, this is a discussion that would have only been held by two or three close friends around a water cooler. To be truthful, I don't know whether the Chairman is charismatic enough to lead this change. However, listening to this discussion, I do know that this company has changed."

Fifth, on the occasion of a benchmarking visit by three representatives from another major firm, the Chairman was advised that he and the guests would attend his debrief session with a Renewal Series class. During the session, people asked the Chairman about such dicey questions as affirmative action goals, business decisions, etc. After the session, the external guests were asked what they thought about the session. The senior person related that they could not believe it. In particular, they could not imagine such a session being accomplished in their own organization because people would not have the courage to ask such questions, the culture would not tolerate it, and the Chairman himself would not allow it. They were advised that it had taken four years of effort to redirect the corporate culture.

Sixth, one senior manager from the Canadian operations remarked to the author that one of the differences he found in the culture now was that people "passed books around to each other" for good ideas. This is related to the event of the senior management team of the Exploration and Production sector (when it was so named) spending part of their staff agenda on day to discuss a popular book on the topic of accountability. However, many tasks went undone and under-accomplished in the eyes of the senior leaderships. Figures 11 and 12 show what they felt were weaknesses and areas for improvement. The information in these figures highlight the fact that for all the strengths of the AMLC Renewal Series, there were organizational needs still being unmet.

Figure 11 demonstrates that the perception was that there was not enough follow-up and reinforcement of what was learned and that

Figure 11:   Perceived Weaknesses—Ideas vs. Skill Building

- Not capturing the best of early learning and sharing that foundation as the top change.
- After first few years follow-up did not happen.
- Don't get reinforcement on what's learned at the AMLC back in the workplace (key concepts—ABM, ACP, etc.).
  1. No integration of themes (middle years seem to be the "flavor of the month" and not connected to each other).
  2. Not enough reinforcement around change management. No roadmap to reach objective of daily tactical issues (clarify roles, accountability, strategic communication, establish key performance indicators, feedback mechanisms).
- Have not changed fast enough (competitors change faster).
  1. Last couple of years were mostly vocabulary. The action has moved to the organizations due to the pace of change.
  2. Different part of the organization in different stages of evolution. Overall, solutions can become ineffective/inefficient—not really a "WE"—all as one.

the L&D training simply did not cause the organization to change fast enough. The irony that the Renewal Series had "become the flavor of the month" in the later years is that the AMLC staff had undertaken a major assessment to prevent just that. As a result of their major needs assessment, they developed a series of four core themes: General Management, Strategic Management, Change Management and Leadership to guide program design and better meet the needs of the participants. These themes were the result of the major needs assessment and reengineering of program design to provide the relevance and focus that the participants felt was missing.

Figure 12 shows one of the major tensions—the issue of ideas vs. skills. From the first year on, there was a constant struggle to balance how much intellectual content should be present vs. how much skill

Figure 12: Perceived Weaknesses by Senior Leaders After Six Years

---

Learning Focuses on Intellectual Content Not Skill Building

- Where do we build skills?
- AMLC should be accessed earlier in management development/ high potential.
- Currently not focused enough on supervisory development at various stages.
- Not enough external development in addition to AMLC.
- Focus on the absolute good rather than the relative good.
- Do teams get more out of the high level learning or more focused content?
- Too prescriptive.
- Some concepts very frustrating to work with—what does it cost in time and money to implement.
- What is the real focus—does not reinforce key practices.

Training Can Only Accomplish So Much—May Be Expecting Too Much

- Supervisors need to carry some responsibility.

---

building. This issue can be debated at many levels (e.g., education vs. training, action vs. reflection, etc.). The genesis of this tension can result from many beginnings. One root lies in the fact that business people prefer action rather than reflection. Therefore, learning programs that provide models and reflection rather than tools, skills and action can be seen as irrelevant. Another root deals with the needs that are being met. It is easier to provide a learning experience that meets a clearly focused set of needs. Recall in earlier paragraphs that the goals of the Renewal process were many and varied. As such, people who desire specific answers were not satisfied. Additionally, the audience represented the broadest spectrum of participants across management ranks. Therefore, programs were designed to meet the multitude of potential needs rather than very focused goals. All of these reasons can lead to the dilution of the effectiveness of the learning experience over time.

The concerns reflected in Figure 12 show how this dilemma played out in the minds of the senior managers. The Renewal Series could not effectively handle all the expectations that were being laid on it during the rapidly changing period for the corporation.

Learning and Learning Organizations

Was Amoco a Learning Organization?

Certainly many programs within the Learning Structure were seen by many as providing value and helping Amoco become a learning organization. Amoco was benchmarked over two dozen times for its Renewal Series. Data reveal that people had "takeaways" that were important to them. For example, senior managers advised the author that people changed as a result of Renewal Series experiences and that change was reflected in their behavior. A major business unit (Amoco Power Resources) was conceived at the Learning Center. Leaders of business units changed philosophy ("line of sight" concept for performance appraisal) at the Learning Center and implemented the ideas back in the business unit (e.g., Norway). Systematic and anecdotal evidence suggests that good things happened.

Figure 13 shows that participants felt that the Renewal Series was having an impact. These data collected from questions on biographical forms from participants attending their second program indicated that they were seeing changes occurring throughout the organization.. Participants sensed that there was more empowerment, sense of management commitment and strategic planning taking place. These are all positive indicators of change.

Was There an Architecture to Guide the Learning?

Certainly, Amoco developed an architecture that gave it some guiding focus to create a learning organization. The Renewal Series staff conducted a needs assessment each year prior to developing the next

Figure 13:   Content Analysis of Perceptions Regarding Renewal

1993 - 1994 AMLC Participants: Other Indicators

Changes Indicative of Renewal Occurring in Amoco

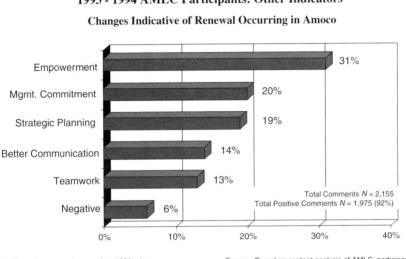

Total Comments *N* = 2,155
Total Positive Comments *N* = 1,975 (92%)

* Percentages sum to more than 100% since
participants could mention more than one change.

Source: Based on content analysis of AMLC participants'
comments in Program II on biographical form.

program. This assessment was included in presentations and discussions with the senior management team. The AMLC supported the other parts of the organization and was market driven. The L&D Framework and the Shared Services Framework guided the thinking, programs and actions of the learning center staff regarding what they offered to the organization.

Was the Organization a Learning Organization?

This is the most difficult question. The answer is somewhat of an enigma. There was learning but as frequently as it was seen as positive it was also seen as misguided or not helpful. Therefore, the learning was within individuals and business units and not evenly distributed throughout the entire organization.

What Allowed the Organization to be Successful?

Where success occurred, clearly people at all levels were involved and saw results. Learning that is interesting can last for a while but to be maintained it must be seen as impacting the business. There are dozens if not hundreds of stories as to how learning impacted the business. However, when the stock price does not go up, faith begins to crumble and people begin looking for the next solution. At my most disillusioned moments, many of the comments of Eileen Shapiro in *Fad Surfing in the Boardroom* were relevant (Shapiro, 1995). Shapiro provides a nice account of senior managers expecting "silver bullets" from too many temporary management ideas/fads.

Other Learning

The period of 1991 through 1999 was turbulent but no more so than for any other business in many ways. The learning structure at Amoco had to both withstand the external industry and internal corporate turbulence while providing programs that assisted in the resolution of the turbulence and change. A summary of this story is a multi-faceted one.

First, there was the creation of a new corporate educational function to help achieve the concept of renewal within the corporation. This organization had modest success as shown by the data.

Second, there was the consolidation of all learning functions (and OD functions) under one organization (the Organization Capability Group, OCG). This organization had its own internal learning and struggles. In particular, as Sandy Quesada and her colleague, Allison Rossett used to say that L&D folks and OD folks are "siblings but not twins" often "separated at birth," (Rossett, 1996). Understanding the different needs, goals, models and structures of these two groups became an interesting challenge as we built and operated the OCG.

Third, there was the creation of Shared Services, which caused all service functions to be a "business within a business." This led to a series of internal changes as we tried to get the roles correct for the unique interaction of the two different functions of the OD and

L&D groups. This led to all kinds of issues related to pay, organizational status, roles (internal partnering often was more difficult than partnering with our clients), responsibilities, relationship with clients, etc. These were internal struggles. To our clients, we were now a "fee-for-service" group that competed with "free" service (see below). Therefore, we were seen as overpriced (e.g., rates that started at a range of $800–$1,200 per day and ended after several years at $1,200–$1,600 per day). Clients would continually ask us for detailed itemized bills of expenses, when they would sign a three-line invoice from an external consulting firm for hundreds of thousands of dollars without question. Working out a billing system led to an incredible unproductive waste of time.

Fourth, there were struggles with other organizations. In particular, the "quality/continuous improvement/progress" function of the organization, which basically followed the Baldrige model, represented a competing organization that operated under a different model. That is, while the OCG fell under the Shared Services organization and became a fee-for-service group, the "Progress" (i.e., quality, continuous improvement, Baldrige) organization was represented by people who were members of the staff of each business unit.

Fifth, while there were two major consulting and L&D organizations in the corporation (OCG and Progress/Baldrige), this did not stop business units from creating L&D activities on their own or from going outside for consulting assistance. This made the game more difficult.

Sixth, the industry and the corporation came under stress and this led to pressure on everyone.

In sum, these were but a few of the problems. They got in the way but they did not stop the OCG from being successful by the standard of becoming self-sufficient (recovering its costs). Additionally, there were some excellent successes within various business units.

Some of these have been mentioned throughout this chapter (e.g., new business unit envisioned at the Renewal Series and later approved; executive advising the author at a Renewal Series program that they had taken millions of dollars of costs out of their business the week his team met at the learning center to go through the program; executive advising the author that concepts of empowerment and diversity learned at the AMLC Renewal Series resulted in a multi-million dollar savings on a project in Egypt; the systematic follow-up of team projects in program four which showed that 61% of the teams made substantial business/financial progress on the problems they brought to the Renewal Series to work on, etc.).

Overall, it was a fascinating ride. The concept of using learning to create and sustain change and in the process to create a learning organization is one more easily written about than accomplished. Our experience gave us glimpses of attaining this goal. However, in the end, the quest was eclipsed by the BP acquisition. While the Learning Centers, the learning system and the AMLC were "shuttered" by the new owners, all learning was distributed to those who spent time in the quest, and their new organizations and their endeavors are the richer for it.

Endnotes

1. It is important to note that the group is not called a Human Resource Development Group. That was a conscious and wise decision by Dr. Carol Dubnicki, then head of the group. It was her thinking that titling the group as HRD would cause people to surmise that the role of the OCG was only to deal with individuals instead of both individuals and the total organization depending on the unit in question.

2. It is a fascinating discussion to see how resources were originally allocated to the OCG. While the goal was to put people where they best fit, these initial personnel allocation decisions were often made for personal and political reasons by the senior HR community that left the OCG with an immediately difficult

problem of categorizing the resources and skills available and balancing the disparate salary structure inherited from the former major business units (e.g., Chemical, Refining and Marketing, Exploration and Production, and Corporate).

3. To make this work, it took the vitality of the Senior Learning Consultants (Linda Petchenik, Gretcha Flinn, Jeanne O'Connor Green, Mike Venn and Gloria Schlein-Polard) and the support of my two colleagues on the consulting side (Mark Wojcik and Gary Myszkowski).

4. Bruce McBratney's insightful categorization of the critical L&D categories and Linda Petchenik's development of the basic model under which all of the Learning Centers were operated.

5. Beau Rezendes, Senior Learning Consultant in the OCG, was primarily responsible for the *Employee Resource Guide*. This guide proved to be a model of both the hardcopy and online internal documents. It was updated annually and provided information on programs related to the Amoco leadership competencies, feedback from Amoco managers/leaders who had attended the various programs and hot links to online services to locate more information on the programs in the guide or other programs of interest. The guide was produced yearly and distributed to HR managers to use in their succession planning and human resource development work.

This chapter was contributed by Dr. William Clover, who was Chief Learning Officer at Amoco from 1991 to 1999. He is now CLO at Williams Company in Tulsa, Oklahoma.

CHAPTER 7

Imbedding Learning in the Organization: The Coca-Cola Story

Introduction

I continue to struggle with the concept of a learning organization even as I have worked within organizations to build them. While I subscribe to the vision of an organization that can continuously learn from its experience in order to create its future, I believe that the characteristics of the "learning organization" that have been discussed in the literature are in many ways impossible to achieve in a large, diverse and particularly global business environment. Organizational politics, the lack of an accepted new paradigm for leadership, distance, bias for action, and local culture all act as forces that inhibit the formation of the global business that functions as a learning organization.

I do, however, believe that people in organizations can make the strategic choice to learn if, in fact, they see learning as a capability that will help close the gap between where they want to be and where they are today. This is the approach to learning that we took at The Coca-Cola Company. Leaders must make the explicit choice to build the learning capability of their organizations. And they must make that choice based on knowledge of what learning can do to help the organization achieve its aspirations. Asking "do you want to become a learning organization?" held very little currency at Coca-Cola. Asking "do you want to be clear as a leadership team on what you are trying to create in your business; do you want to understand why you get the results you do today; and do you want to be more effective as a team in changing what really needs to be changed," generated much more interest.

Guiding Ideas

My job, in the first year I was with the company, was to work with then COO Doug Ivester to define a destination for learning in the company, develop a strategy to reach it and put the infrastructure and capability in place to execute the strategy. It was, in other words, to build the architecture. This effort, in fact, took a year. I believe that there is no standard formula or strategy for building learning as a capability in a business. The right strategy is so dependent on the culture of the company, what it is trying to accomplish and what the CEO will ultimately stand for and be a leader of, that it pays to understand these things clearly before you begin. At Coca-Cola, this meant interviews and discussions with senior management about what was important to them, discussions with the human resource organization about what had worked in the past and what hadn't and why, development of an initial concept paper, sharing of that concept paper with line management globally, and six months of conversation with Doug Ivester to understand as much as I could about the business and come to a shared vision of what learning would be at Coca-Cola. I remember thinking at the time that all of this was taking too long, but in retrospect it was the perfect lesson in "slowing down to speed up." Without the clarity gained in those six months we would have never accomplished what we did in the following three years.

The first piece of this architecture was put in place with the decision that what we wanted out of the learning effort was a "greater capacity for value producing action." We would stay away from tying the effort to courses or programs and center our work on the outcome we were after—higher levels of capability that would ultimately build shareowner value.

Five guiding principles then were the foundation of the learning strategy at Coca-Cola:

- Connect all "learning work" directly to the business.
- Insert it into key business processes through relevant projects, not learning programs.
- Use the projects to build learning capability in the business units as you deliver on clear business outcomes.
- Do not sell learning or demand it of the operating units.
- Focus on leaders who were "ready." Add value to the business and others will follow.

Four guiding ideas then drove the thinking around the architecture:

- **Learning is connected to business strategy in the development of capabilities.** Understanding that learning is intended to help organizations build the capabilities they need to execute their strategies and meet their goals, our architecture would have to include people, methods and tools to make this linkage explicit.
- **It is important to understand why.** Recognizing that learning was about being as concerned about why we get results as about the results themselves, we would have to have both people and processes that introduced and built systems thinking and productive conversation skills in a practical way.
- **Knowledge is a valuable global asset.** Understanding that while markets and people may be unique, experience can be transferred around the world. We would have to have an approach to knowledge management that was about people not just technology.
- **Individual development and organizational learning reinforce each other.** Recognizing the connection between individual learning and development and organizational learning, our infrastructure would have to include strong capability in both and a logical connection between the two.

Infrastructure: The Learning Consortium

Given the direction we were taking, it was clear that this effort required an infrastructure to support and act as a catalyst to work with the operating units. This infrastructure became the Coca-Cola Learning Consortium. The Consortium was to be a project-based consulting organization built on a strategic framework but driven by the needs of the business. Its purpose was to help business units build their capability to strengthen the quality of human and intellectual capital in the Coca-Cola system through the use of learning principles, frameworks, methods and tools.

The thinking behind the Consortium as a project-based organization was actually quite simple. First, in order for this "learning stuff" to connect with the business, we needed credible business people attached to each of the operating groups and corporate functions to understand and see the link to strategy and capability. Second, once this linkage was understood, we needed people with practical experience in a number of "learning areas" to design and execute projects, contracted by the business units that would make this linkage real and add value to the business while building learning capability in the business.

So **we created the position of Director of Learning Strategy (DLS)** for each operating group and function in the company and recruited high performing line and functional managers, as well as a few external strategy consultants, to fill those roles. These individuals were to stay in the DLS role for up to three years and then move into management within their business unit. We taught the DLSs an approach to strategy development that was grounded in the disciplines of organizational learning. They could use this approach (see Figure 1) with their clients to think through the connections between their clients' business strategy, the capabilities they needed to execute their strategy and the role that learning could play in helping them develop those capabilities. This thinking could then be translated into a learning plan for the unit broken into projects with clear outcomes linked to the business strategy.

Figure 1: The Breakthrough Model

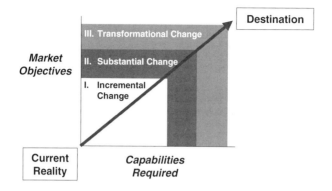

The projects would be scoped, designed and executed by four small consulting units in the Consortium. Units of five to seven individuals were built in the areas of learning skills (the five disciplines), knowledge management, individual competency development and training. (See Table 1 for description of each unit.) Each unit was charged with defining the link between its functional discipline and the strategic framework that guided our work, and creating the methods and tools that would be the basis of our work with the operating units. These methods and tools would allow the people in the Consortium to work and communicate effectively with each other and eventually allow us to replicate the skills we had in networks in the operating units.

The Consulting Units

I've been asked many times why I chose to design the Consortium around the four functional disciplines of learning skills, knowledge management, competency development and training. First it was consistent and reinforcing of the guiding ideas. But why those guiding ideas? I believe there is an organizational lifecycle to learning that becomes even more pronounced when you think about learning in the context of development of capability in a business. The learning disciplines, like shared vision and systems thinking, are key

Table 1:   Consulting Unit Purpose and Methods, Processes and Tools

Unit and Purpose	Methods, Processes and Tools
Learning Skills: Builds skills that enable the business unit and its partners to reach clarity on what they want to achieve in the business and what keeps them from doing it today so that they can create the results that matter to them.	**Methods** for connecting work in the five disciplines to key processes and strategic issues in the business. **Process** for developing learning skills consultants could apply with leadership teams. **Process** for bringing teams from awareness, to understanding, trial and application of learning skills. **Tools** to support the Kolb learning cycle (e.g., after action review).
Knowledge Management: Works with groups, teams and organizations to understand what knowledge is most critical to the successful implementation of their strategies and how this knowledge can be best acquired, developed, transferred and applied	Definition of the knowledge management **process**. **Methodology** for defining and identifying knowledge critical to business unit strategy. **Methods** and **tools** for capturing and sharing knowledge. Workshops to teach the knowledge management **process**. **Tools** for team room design.
Competency Development: Builds models, frameworks and tools that enable business units to understand what distinguishes high performing individuals and how to recruit, develop and retain individuals that have the necessary knowledge, attitudes and behaviors.	Competency models. **Methods** for determining which competencies are most critical. Targeted selection guides for general management. Competency development guides. Programs to develop coaching skills.
Training: Works with line management and training and development organizations to design a training strategy that is directly related to their business goals and to use or create learning experiences that lead to measurable results.	**Methodology** for training strategy. Curriculum for managers. Quick books for design and development. **Tools** for measuring training effectiveness.

to a leadership team's ability to create a vision for their business and understand the gap between that vision and their current reality. It is clarity around that gap that should drive their strategy. Once the team has defined a strategy, knowledge management becomes a very practical issue. As the team begins to consider how it will keep track of the results it is getting from its strategy and, more importantly, why it is getting them, knowledge development, sharing and application provide a basis for learning and refinement of the strategy. Once the strategy becomes a way of doing business, it becomes evident that some individuals execute more successfully than others. It is natural then to ask why they are more successful. What competencies distinguish high performers and how do we get more of them? Finally, skills need to be institutionalized and training comes into play. Each time a strategy is redesigned, this cycle begins again. Having seen this occur over and over again, I decided to broaden the scope of the Consortium to include the skills and disciplines that could see a business through the entire cycle.

The consulting units were based on a shared vision and commitment to hire the best leadership we possibly could in each area and ask them to create a capability that would connect the theories and methods of their discipline to the business issues and strategies of The Coca-Cola Company. Given that most of these areas and many of the people in the consulting units were new to the company, this required a significant learning period. During the first year of operation, a significant amount of time was spent in talking with line managers, understanding issues, describing what we could do to help and working on projects with leaders who were willing to experiment with us.

Some projects went forward and others did not, but by the end of the first year of operation, each consulting unit had some real experience with how its area of expertise related both to the larger learning strategy and to the needs of the business. Each then refined its business plan, articulating the theory behind its work, how the unit would work with the business, what services it would provide and how it would add value to the business. This included definition of the additional skills, methods, processes and tools that would be needed to fulfill the plan. Over the next year, these were developed while we continued project work with the operating units, allowing us to learn about application through experience. Refinement was a continuous process, often in conjunction with a business unit. Examples of the kinds of processes, methods and tools developed are shown in Table 1.

The Strategic Framework Behind the Director of Learning Strategy

Methods and tools also had to be developed to support the Directors of Learning Strategy. This was particularly important given the choice to hire business people and teach them about learning rather than hire learning people and teach them about business. The DLSs were to be the "translators" from the strategy of the business to the learning methods and tools that could accelerate execution. The basis of their work was a strategic framework called the Breakthrough Model. A schematic of the Breakthrough Model is shown in Figure 1. The model is fundamentally a tool for managers that asks them to be clear in their thinking about the results they want in their business and what their organizations must be able to do over time to achieve them. Learning skills, disciplines and tools are used with leadership teams to increase the quality of the input to the model. When management teams work with the model, they connect learning directly to strategy.

The Breakthrough Model is based on four fundamental beliefs about strategy:

■ **Good strategy requires a clear picture of both what you want to create and what you have today.** Leaders must be able to articulate a destination for their business that describes the results they will achieve, in the market and as an organization, by the end of a defined timeframe. They must also be able to say why this destination truly matters. And they must do both with enough texture and clarity that others understand how they can contribute. Equally important is the leader's ability to understand not only where the organization is today, with regard to this destination, but also why (i.e. current reality). This is important for two reasons. First, it is difficult for people to connect to a "stretch" destination if they do not have faith that their leaders understand today's reality. Second, unless both destination and current reality are clear, the gap that must be closed ultimately by strategy is not clear. This is the reason why many strategies miss the mark and fall victim to forces at play in the organization.

■ **Sustainable growth comes from the development of capabilities that allow an organization to see opportunities and capture them.** All companies in an industry are presented with the same level of market opportunity. What distinguishes one company from another is its ability to see those opportunities and act on them. In other words, competitive advantage comes from having the right capabilities to move more quickly than others do in the market time after time.

■ **A brilliant market strategy is greatly hindered by the lack of capability to execute.** It has always struck me how much time is spent in corporate business planning on "what we are going to do" and " what that will do for growth and profit" and how little time is spent on "what we have to be able to do" in order to make any of it happen. This framework asks the manager to clearly see the gap between the results he/she wants to achieve and what is achievable today and then focuses on the capabilities required to execute. The development of capability becomes an integral part of the plan as the manager thinks about what has to happen in terms of people, process, knowledge and environment for the strategy to be executed. In doing this, the timing of results becomes more realistic. The development of capability takes time.

■ **All strategies strive towards a destination but most are staged in their execution.** While we live in a time when "business revolution" and changing the rules of the game are the stuff of success stories, the simple fact that most strategies are about building something or changing something requires that a manager think about what he/she will accomplish by when. This is what "staging" means. The breakthrough model asks the manager to lay out a path to close the gap between what is desired and what is. To do this, the manager must first think through what results will be achieved at each stage (i.e. market objectives) and then what is required to achieve those results at progressively greater levels of organizational change—incremental, substantial and transformational. Even if the manager decides to ultimately skip a stage, this thought process allows him/her to accelerate progress in a much more thoughtful way.

The Projects

The job of the DLS was to guide an operating unit's management team through the Breakthrough Model with the help of learning skills consultants. Working through the model to its completion draws on all five of Senge's learning disciplines. Identifying and ultimately developing capability, in most cases, draws on knowledge management, competency development and training as well as other functional disciplines in context of the unit's strategy (see Figure 2). In fact, some units had more patience for the exercise than others did but the thinking took hold in many operating units. In those cases, once priority capabilities were identified, the DLS developed a learning plan that defined projects that the unit would undertake with assistance from the Consortium.

In reality not all project work developed through this path. Some client organizations took on the systematic approach of the Breakthrough Model in their business plans and major initiatives for the perspective it provided in planning. In this case the Consortium supported their efforts to define a destination or understand current reality. In other cases, individual business units called on the DLS for help on a particular business issue like the need to improve the

Figure 2:   Breakthrough Model with Learning Disciplines

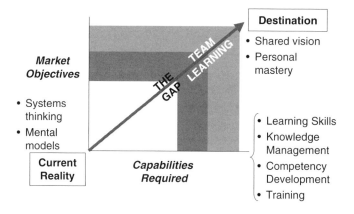

effectiveness of the leadership team, improve company/bottler alignment or understand why results were what they were in the unit. In this case, the DLS would work to understand the issue, design a project and bring the right combination of skills from the consulting units to reach the business outcomes desired by the client organization. Table 2 provides an illustration of the kinds of projects that a DLS would undertake in an operating group or division. This example is based on actual work performed by the Consortium.

Other units focused on learning projects in support of major business initiatives. Many of these initiatives stemmed from the need to enhance critical capabilities, for example, customer understanding. Work on this particular capability drew on literally every part of the Consortium. Individual DLS's worked with leadership teams to identify what this capability meant in their markets. The learning skills group was called on to work with account teams and their customers in a joint planning exercise based on the Breakthrough Model. Knowledge management worked with units to begin to share, or capture and leverage knowledge about the customer. The competency development group undertook behavioral event interviews with key customer contacts around the system to identify those competencies that differentiated high performers from average

Table 2:   Examples of Learning Consortium Projects

Project Outcome	Description	Consulting Support Required
Develop a destination for the system in the XYZ division.	Work with the leadership team of the division and the bottler to clarify a destination for this planning period. Introduce the concepts of shared vision and mental models. Work on productive conversation skills. Build teams ability to understand each others perspective and assumptions about the market.	Learning skills
Current reality—understand why the system is not able to fulfill the demand in the market for our products.	Interview individuals from the region, the bottler and customer organizations as the basis of a systems dynamics analysis of why we cannot fulfill demand. Train company personnel to participate in the interviews and the analysis so there is capability to do this kind of work again.	Director of Learning Strategy Learning skills
Understand what contributed to the success of a specific channel marketing plan. Capture the learnings so that the process can be repeated by other channel marketing groups.	Conduct an after action review with this team to understand what worked, what didn't and why. Document the process and the environment in which the process worked for use by other teams. Coach this team to leverage their learnings to a next planning cycle.	Learning skills Knowledge management Possibly training

Table 2: Examples of Learning Consortium Projects (*Continued*)

Project Outcome	Description	Consulting Support Required
Understand why a competitor was able to increase its market share dramatically and transfer this knowledge to the marketing organization.	Work with both the marketing and HR organization to capture knowledge about what the competitor did and why it was effective from the company, bottler, customer and consumer perspective. Build skills of the HR organization in knowledge capture and transfer.	Knowledge management
Understand why our interactions with customers are not producing the desired results. Define the skills our people need and how to develop them.	Focus on one major customer. Work with the account team to develop its ability to listen to the customer and understand the structures that get in the way of success. Document those structures. Work with the account team to develop a joint plan of action with the customer. Based on these findings and global work on customer competencies, recommend to management an approach to skill development.	Director of Learning Strategy Learning skills Competency development
Provide a framework and approach to the development of division leadership.	Reacquaint group leadership with the company's competency model. Agree on how the model relates to the group's business plan. Administer 360° feedback on the model to division presidents and work with them and the Group President on their development plans.	Competency development

performers. Global training worked to support a global customer curriculum. The DLS continued to be the person responsible for connecting this work to the business.

Finally, some clients became invested in a particular area of learning (e.g. learning skills, knowledge management) and the consultants that worked with them. These managers would work with those consultants to build this particular kind of learning capability in their unit believing that it provided enough enduring value to invest in the capability itself. In this case, the DLS was involved in and was kept informed about the work.

The DLS Role

While I am very proud of the work we were able to accomplish with the DLSs, I will tell you that things were not nearly as orderly as they appeared. The strategy of putting business people into these roles and developing their understanding of learning was the right one. It definitely made the concept of learning more tangible, practical and acceptable to the organization. But here's the tradeoff. We took very competent, high-performing people in their original fields and made them immediately incompetent in their new roles. While we did about three weeks of up-front training with the DLSs, no realistic amount of up-front training can truly prepare people for these roles. They have to get into the business and begin to work with line management. Now, of course, line management also had very limited experience with the concepts behind the work. So, in effect, we had a nine-month period where both the DLS and the clients were learning and experimenting. The downside of this approach was early frustration. The upside was that the DLSs did not try to impose a predetermined learning agenda on the business units. The agenda was co-created.

Over time the competencies required of a DLS began to be evident as we gained more experience with the role. Knowledge of the business remained critical but other competencies were equally important including tolerance for ambiguity, ability to exert personal influence, judgment and common sense, the ability to think both systemically and strategically, and the ability to build value-based relationships. The learning here is that while some of these can be developed on the job and others can be coached, many are attributes that must be part of the individual when they are recruited.

Had I to recruit and train DLSs again, I would do several things differently. First, I would put more emphasis on the role as a leadership development role. This was the hidden bonus for the DLS in that as they learned more about learning and became more competent in their job, their knowledge of themselves grew and their leadership ability increased. Second, I would reformulate their training to focus not only on the strategic framework they followed but also more intensely on their individual learning skills. While I would still do up-front training to acclimate them to their new role, I would modularize other training interspersed with periods of client work. (Although, in reality this is very difficult to do.) Finally, I would stagger the start dates of the DLSs, bringing on two or three at a time, providing them with a more individualized approach to development and coaching by more experienced DLSs. This is, in fact, what we moved to as new DLSs were brought on board.

The Consortium Operating Model

After the first year, the operating model for the Consortium was very similar to that of an external consulting firm. We had both a vision and purpose for the unit. We had a business plan. We had yearly objectives for which we were accountable. We had standards for productivity. We had business systems that helped us collectively understand the work we were doing and what we were learning. We had development programs for our people. We had relationships to manage and we had pressure to add value. Projects came into the unit either through the DLSs as part of their plan or directly to the consulting units. They were scoped, staffed, designed and implemented.

Community Building

Like most other project-based businesses, we had to juggle the work of the projects and the development of the organization. In the midst of deadlines and daily crises, it is easy to forget that great communities devoted to a common purpose do great work. Over time we experimented with and adopted a number of activities and tools to build our community. For example, we put together an orientation guide to the Consortium documenting our vision and purpose, the year's objectives, our client service philosophy, and the purpose and work of each group in the Consortium. We arranged "lunch and learns" so that consulting groups could become familiar with each others' work. We held Consortium-wide development days where we would work together on a particular issue or learn from a particular project. We implemented a project management system that allowed any member of the Consortium to see what work was going on and how it was progressing.

We also implemented a somewhat nontraditional approach to performance measurement and appraisal. Each member of the Consortium was evaluated based on a common scorecard. The scorecard had four cells: client satisfaction, living the values of the Consortium, contribution to building capability in the Consortium and applied individual learning. Each cell was individually weighted and scored. Fifty percent of the overall score was based on satisfaction ratings from clients. While at times it was very difficult to get client feedback, this weighting served to focus the organization on why we existed—to provide value to the business. The values section of the scorecard was based on 360° feedback on a set of values that the Consortium had identified as the way we wanted to work. These values are shown in Figure 3. The capability section of the scorecard was based on the individual's contribution to Consortium-wide or consulting unit projects to build methods and tools that enhanced our work. Sometimes this kind of work gets left behind as individuals are consumed by client work. We could not afford for this to happen. Finally, the applied learning section of the scorecard

Figure 3:   Consortium Values

CCLC Values

We achieve the Learning Consortium's purpose through CCLC associates, individually and collectively, demonstrating supporting values and behaviors.

The Coca-Cola Learning Consortium acts with professionalism and uncompromised integrity in a fun work environment where the following values and behaviors are demonstrated:

Personal Responsibility:
1. Produces accurate, timely and high quality (i.e., fit-for-purpose) work.
2. Follows through on assignments from and commitments to clients and CCLC members.
3. Give and seeks honest and constructive feedback.
4. Manages differences/conflicts in a timely, direct and candid manner.
5. Assumes personal responsibility for actions, issues and outcomes.

Respect And Value Others:
6. Actively seeks and considers others ideas, views and inputs.
7. Suspends judgment while seeking to make others and own thinking explicit.
8. Acknowledges and thanks others for results and efforts.
9. Is consistent and truthful in actions and words.
10. Handles disagreement and feedback on difficult issues in an open, fair and non-defensive manner.

Value-Added Impact:
11. Capitalizes on both existing thinking/solutions and new ideas to meet client needs.
12. Understands and is guided by the organization's, client's and CCLC's business destinations.
13. Aligns work (i.e., content, scope, approach, pace) to current client and business situations.
14. Uses language appropriate to the business and the given audience.
15. Presents recommendations when surfacing problems/issues.

Enhancing Collective Capability:
16. Keeps people up-to-date and provides access to relevant information and learning.
17. Understands how one's individual efforts and actions impact the CCLC's work, and acts to ensure coordinated/seamless services to clients.
18. Responds to calls for help from CCLC members.
19. Utilizes opportunities and coaching to build skills/competencies in CCLC members.
20. Takes an active role (i.e., suggesting, participating, identifying opportunities) in helping to enhance the CCLC's effectiveness.

focused on the individual's personal learning objectives for the year and whether or not they progressed on those objectives. Scores in each area were combined into an overall score that linked to compensation. The scorecard led to good conversations between the associate and their manager about their performance during the year. It also served as a concrete symbol of what was important to our success.

Managing and Leveraging Resources

I have said that the Consortium ran much like a consulting firm with one very important exception—fees were not tied to contracts. In fact after the second year of operation, the operating units were allocated expenses for services from the Consortium but this was done as part of the budget exercise rather than on a project by project basis. This one difference had a major impact on our ability to allocate resources effectively. Time was spent working with units, designing projects and at times even beginning work only to have that work moved or changed for other priorities. While this is the case for all consulting entities, inside or out, it affected the Consortium dramatically for two reasons. First, we ran very lean. Only five to seven consultants were available in each area to serve more than twenty divisions and a number of corporate functions globally. Second, we found that once work began in earnest with a unit, it tended to continue as the unit sought to build its own capability. So, the complexity of scheduling continuing and new work with a limited number of resources and changing priorities on the part of the operating units became a real challenge.

We took on this challenge in a number of ways. First, we instituted a management team for the Consortium comprised of the Directors of each of the consulting units and the Lead Director of learning strategy. This group had both a strategic and a tactical role. The management team:

- Developed the three year destination for the Consortium and the objectives for each year.

- Reviewed progress on objectives and made adjustments.
- Developed guiding principles for providing service to clients.
- Agreed on business systems (e.g. project management, knowledge management and time recording) to support our work.
- Guided the overall development strategy for Consortium consultants.
- Understood where we were collectively with each client organization, why, and what should be done about it.
- Agreed on priorities for resource allocation and stayed on top of them as timing of commitments shifted.

As we became accustomed to the rhythms of each of the operating units and the working styles of the DLSs, this group was able to make progress in managing the resource allocation issue, but the issue remained. Recognizing that we could not merely manage our way out of the issue and that we were in a way acting as a limit to our own success, we began to examine how our operating model needed to change. As I have described, the first year of operation for the Consortium was one of experimentation and method and tool development. The second year was devoted to project work for clients and the continuation of tool development. At the end of that year, as we saw demand grow for our services and our resource issues escalate, we sharpened our focus on building capability in each Consortium consulting area in the operating units.

We targeted those business units that had done a number of projects with us in a particular area with the goal of enabling them to be self-sufficient. Each consulting unit developed their own plan for building capability. They developed the business case, identified units where the leadership had experience and commitment to the work, and connected with individuals who were interested in developing their own capability. They then designed methods for building capability that ranged from quickbooks, to coaching, to workshops, to project work and residential programs that would be sponsored and supported by the business units. By focusing on building capability in the operating units along with direct project work, we were able to begin to leverage Consortium tools and people for greater impact. Should we have done this earlier? I don't think so. By waiting, we were able to provide a service in which the business saw value rather than sell programs that they did not yet understand.

What We Accomplished

I have told you a lot about the architecture for learning that we put in place at Coca-Cola. I have also described what the Consortium did and why we did it and the kinds of work that came from it. What did we accomplish as a result of it? I believe we accomplished several things. Some are more important than others. I will let you be the judge of which, in fact, were more important.

First, we gave individuals, groups and teams the experience of what learning feels like in an organization, insight into how it happens and, perhaps most importantly, how it can relate to the business. Second, we taught leaders that learning is a strategic choice—not something that just happens. Third, we introduced into the organization tools that facilitate learning, like productive conversation, systems thinking for understanding complex situations, processes for identifying and transferring knowledge, and models for individual development. In some business units, we changed behaviors. These units began to view the process of debriefing, for example, not as a search for the guilty but as a process of discovery that informed future actions and led to better results. They also began to appreciate feedback to individual employees as a line management process for enhancing organizational performance and training as a way to accelerate successful strategy. Finally, we helped several teams and a number of organizations actually move toward being learning organizations in that they were able to understand how to use their collective experience and the methods and tools we had provided to create their future.

Accelerators to Progress

Looking back I can identify six major factors that allowed the Consortium to have an impact on the business:

- **Senior level advocacy.** I was very fortunate to have both a CEO and COO as advocates for the work. Both Roberto Goizueta and Doug Ivestor saw the work as important to the future of the business and were willing to both devote resources to it and advocate for it. Most importantly, Doug Ivestor spent those many months with me understanding the logic of the work, its connection to the business and the personal skills required to lead from a learning perspective. He practiced those skills in his interactions with the business units and personally sponsored several projects that gave the Consortium a chance to prove that it deserved the attention of a performance-based organization like Coca-Cola.

- **The Consortium as a place to learn about learning.** I have described the Consortium as a catalyst for learning in the organization. It was also a catalyst for learning for the people directly involved in the work. This was new work. Roles were ambiguous. Skills needed to be developed. Successes needed to be leveraged. Failures needed to be understood. People needed to be supported when things were going too fast or too slow. The Consortium provided this environment for the individuals who chose to be pioneers in learning at Coca-Cola and, as such, it accelerated our progress. I have been asked why I did not just put the DLSs into the operating units and functions. My answer is that they would not have learned anything about learning. They would have fallen back on their existing strengths and become the clients rather than educated advocates for the work.

- **Linkage to the business planning process.** The business planning process must be the central learning process of a business organization. Otherwise, any learning effort will have very little credibility. Businesses must continuously learn from both their successful and unsuccessful strategies in order to survive and grow. Further, this process, of any in the business, should be the place where aspiration, understanding complexity and collaboration are present—three capabilities that are essential to learning. With this in mind, one of the projects that Doug Ivestor sponsored asked the question "Why do we get only the level of aspiration that we do in our business plans?" Through debriefs and interviews with managers we were able to identify four underlying structures that acted as inhibitors of aspiration in the business planning process. The process was then redesigned and followed for two years to understand whether those structures were indeed falling away and being replaced by those that led to greater aspiration. This project helped our learning effort in several ways. First it provided a practical example of the use of systems thinking to understand why things happen the way they do in an organization. Second, it led to changes in the process that line managers found valuable, giving the work credibility. Third, the business planning process became a place where learning skills were valued; understanding why was essential and the role of capability development began to be apparent.

- **Following a pull strategy.** One of our early guiding principles was to spend the Consortium's time and energy on only those leaders who were ready. This evolved to what we called "working on pull." Working on pull meant that we would not sell our services to the line and we would not require that any unit participate in any of the work. The philosophy behind this strategy was first, that learning was not an act of compliance and if it was perceived as one, it would be just another corporate program. Second, we believed that our limited resources were best spent on those who wanted to move forward. All of us had had the experience of spending too much time and energy trying to convince people that they should become part of the work and having very little time or energy left for those who were ready to move. None of us wanted to repeat that experience. The pull strategy turned out to be a smart way of doing business. While we were always willing to spend time with a leader who wanted to learn more before proceeding, focusing our time and effort where there was real demand for the work allowed us to move more quickly, focus our resources and be relevant to our client base.

- **Focusing on leaders as our clients and business issues as our issues.** Learning can very easily fall prey to the dilemma of being about everything and therefore nothing. In fact when I arrived at Coca-Cola there was a great deal of confusion about what this "learning thing" would be about. Mental models about learning in large business organizations tend to still focus on training and individual development plans. Therefore, the approach that we chose to take, focusing on leaders of business units and how learning can help resolve business issues, was seen as rather unorthodox and even somewhat threatening to some line managers. However, at least in Coca-Cola, it was the right thing to do. If learning is to be a strategic capability in a large hierarchical organization, someone must make the choice to focus on it. While grassroots initiatives can have impact, generally the leader must at least be "for it" if it is to play a real role in how the business runs. There is a much higher probability that leadership will embrace learning if they can see that it will help them resolve the very real issues they face. Certainly at Coca-Cola, this was the case. Not all leaders embraced our work but the client base grew every year and I was always able to say who wanted our work, why and how it was relevant.

- **Building the capability of constituencies in the field.** Learning is not new to most organizations. For years there have been people in corporations under the guise of organizational effectiveness, training, human resources and leadership who work with similar objectives in mind. Enrolling these resources as part of our community and building their capability as part of our strategy helped accelerate our progress and connect us to a field presence that we otherwise would not have had. In time, it also helped us overcome some of the natural tension with the HR organization. In fact, where there was not a natural network in the organization, we worked to create one. This was the case with our local learning skill network. As I described earlier, these networks gave us both leverage and proximity to the business, not to mention helping us to fulfill our objective of building learning capability in the field.

Obstacles to Progress

There were obviously things that inhibited our progress. Some leaders did not see value in spending time and resources on learning as we had defined it. They had other priorities and points of view. While I do not intend to minimize this—obviously it had a profound effect on the effort in the long run—I would like to focus here on those obstacles that are structural to the organization.

- **The propensity to act.** A strength of many companies like The Coca-Cola Company is their bias for action. The focus is on performance and in order to perform one must act. The downside of this bias is the limited appetite for reflection. The tendency is to act, see results and act again without truly understanding why the results were achieved. While we focused heavily on the ability to understand why, existing mental models about what activities were valued and therefore deserved time and attention slowed the learning process down. Further, the tendency to advocate strongly for a point of view rather than to inquire openly about "what happened" is so well ingrained in most businesses that overcoming it takes a great deal of discipline and consistent leadership from the top.
- **The discipline of planning.** Planning to build capability requires time and senior level thought. The framework for learning we put in place at Coke asked leaders to take that time and continue their thinking beyond strategy into what they needed to be able to do to accomplish that strategy and then do it. While this sounds logical and few would argue with it, few executives have taken capability on as a planning task. In most cases, capability is seen as getting the right person for the job. All of us have seen the consequences of expensive hires brought into an environment lacking in the necessary processes,

knowledge and leadership to get the job done. In order for this to change, capability must be a serious strategic thrust in and of itself in the business that goes beyond HR. At the same time the approach to learning must have enough flexibility to allow business units to begin to work with learning concepts to help resolve issues even without a capability plan. We called this "meeting them where they are."

■ **New concepts and language.** Bringing learning concepts into an organization takes time particularly if you want to bring them into the mainstream, beyond the HR organization. Bringing learning language into an organization only takes a second, the time needed for the word to be formed and spoken in a room full of the unwashed. I have learned to be careful with language. While it is true that there are some concepts and ways of working for which there is no comfortable existing business language, one must use new terms judiciously. Words can slow you down and provide a point of controversy that takes away from the work you are trying to accomplish. Leading with analogy, example or story to describe what you are trying to get across and then providing the language to explain a shared experience, I found, is a better start.

■ **Organizational silos.** Our placement of DLSs followed the existing organizational structure—groups, functions, and in some cases, divisions. I believe this was the right thing to do. Introducing new concepts through an organization that is not aligned with the existing one is too much of a double back flip. However, as you start to deal with real systemic issues in the organization or introduce learning concepts and tools into clear strategic priorities, those boundaries get in the way and slow you down. We dealt with this problem through what we called "collective projects." These projects were usually about organization-wide issues and involved a relevant group if not all of the DLSs as well as the consulting staff. They originated either with the CEO or within an operating group. In the latter case, when appropriate, the DLSs worked to leverage the work to their client base.

- **Mental models about corporate.** I envisioned the Consortium as a service organization, neither corporate nor field, based on a value proposition. I actually fought not to have it be a department in corporate until I found out that there was no other way to identify it. The reason why I felt passionate about this was because of many years working in companies as a consultant and seeing the tension between corporate and the field. This tension might, in fact be natural and in some cases healthy, but I did not see how it would, ultimately, enable learning. As a department, we had to find other ways to identify ourselves as a service business. We did this through our operating philosophies and evaluation methodologies but we never really overcame the corporate label with some operating managers.

- **Changes in leadership.** I have said that I believe that the choice to build learning as a capability in an organization is an explicit choice made by leaders. This is, perhaps, most obvious when leadership changes. While you can bring the disciplines, methods and tools of organizational learning to individuals, teams and groups within an organization, if the leader does not chose to lead from a learning perspective, the work is difficult to sustain. It may go "underground." It may remain active within particular teams but, at best, progress slows. In a culture where changes in leadership are frequent and common, this can work both for and against a learning agenda as "learning leaders" move to new areas of responsibility.

Epilogue

I am going to conclude where I began. Introducing learning into a large, diverse, global organization is a struggle. The Learning Consortium at Coca-Cola does not exist anymore. As I have said, the decision to introduce learning into an organization and how it is done is ultimately a leadership decision. In this case, as leadership changed, other priorities took precedence. Was the Consortium a success? It was for the people who worked in it and the managers who implemented and learned from its work. While the architecture has changed, in that the Consortium is no longer fulcrum, the thinking, processes and tools live on in the networks we built, the way many managers approach their work and the continued thinking around organizational and individual capability development. In many ways the Consortium fulfilled its mission as a catalyst. The new architecture for learning can now be created by the new leadership. They have a tremendous headstart.

Judith Rosenblum, who served as Chief Learning Officer at the Coca-Cola Company from 1995 to 2000, contributed this chapter. She is now the Chief Operating Officer at Duke Corporate Education, Inc., Durham, North Carolina.

CHAPTER 8

Reinventing a Company:
The Prudential Financial Story

O n the landscape of the financial sector, a smarter, stronger player has arrived. As of fall, 2002, Prudential Financial nears completion of its first full year on the stock market after many decades as a mutual insurance company. In a year that has rattled many a name corporation, PRU has held its value brilliantly: the stock is equal to its December 2001 opening price, while the S&P 500 is down 20%. How did the Prudential Insurance Company of America become PRU (NYSE), and what did "learning" have to do with it?

From 1997 through 2001, Prudential, the venerable "rock," pried itself from the ranks of the great, ponderous mutual insurers and became a financial services company. In large part, this remarkable transformation was driven by a massive, groundbreaking corporate learning strategy. Led by the Chairman and his executive team, this strategy involved virtually every one of Prudential's 57, 000 U.S. employees. It mobilized many thousands of people toward a new, fresh understanding of the company, its competitive realities and bright future.

Prudential's story shows how corporate learning can propel transformation, and how leaders throughout a company must be both learning's staunchest champions and its greatest beneficiaries. It tells why performance is the core purpose of all corporate learning. Most of all, it tells how your future in business, and mine, is a better one now that corporate learning has come of age.

The Task at Hand

For all their size and muscle, the world's biggest companies are rarely in a steady state. Many have had to deal with the fading away of former glories, and have cut themselves loose from their own traditions in quest of a better place—a better place in the market, in the competitive set, in the eyes of investors and customers.

We faced this at Prudential. Decades of greatness, even dominance, in our core businesses had been achieved during a steady state (now expired) in which predictability and the care of assets under management, instead of earnings growth and efficient use of capital, were the bases for success. Like some other large sectors of the economy (telecommunications, computing) we in financial services now faced new realities: in the lowering of barriers, so that powerful new rivals could enter our business; in the creation, management and movement of information as the "coin of the realm"; in the constant pulse of technology that underlies everything we do; in the dramatic, beneficial changes in customer experience that is the aim of all effort and the test of success.

Cutting loose from the familiar guarantees a wrenching ride. Progress is rarely linear and, for most executives, the job of leading is much tougher. Groans arise from the organization's great middle; formerly docile employees clamor for information about the new realities, then grouse about the news when they get it. Talented managers hoist the banner of change and are chastised for taking risks. The press for execution prompts the search for single point accountabilities, and leads to the discovery that these are alarmingly rare. The fuzzy bonhomie of "teamwork" evaporates under pressure for results; solid performers turn churlish and protective, good people drift away and expenses climb.

Good leaders thrive on these challenges, as the recent history of Prudential Financial shows. Because the basic need was to mobilize a whole organization in a new direction, a learning strategy is woven into the picture in bold colors. The learning job was massive—it touched almost every employee in the company. The tools and techniques were inventive, fresh and risky. The plan of engagement started at the very top of the company and was a nail-biter for all concerned. Our learning organization did its job. But the real story is about our executives, what they did individually and together, to take control of the organization and lead it toward a new place.

Pru Gets Serious About Learning

In early 1997, Chairman Art Ryan moved boldly on the learning front, persuading Canadian banking executive Michele Darling to join Pru and lead Human Resources. In the bargain, he committed to build or purchase a world-class learning center for the company. In turn, an early directive from Ryan to Darling was to "give everyone in the organization an understanding of our mission, strategy and keys to success."

The tone for the next several years was set. Prudential's 57,000 associates were to be well-informed. If possible, they were to be the best-informed employees in the industry. Leaps in performance were to result from local action, the entire company was to excel. The driving force behind change was to be based on marshalling the efforts of the many that saw for themselves the looming peril of the existing state and the rewards of positive change.

Lofty plans give leaders messy tasks. Such an infusion of new information and involvement was much too significant to delegate to "the learning folks." Pru's people would need to see and work with their executives, up close and personal. Yet the shift from traditional management to an "unleashing" of the organization called for a new kind of executive performance. Yes, the company's huge Operations and Systems group, Pru's back office, held some massive meetings in which new mobilization techniques were developed. But this involved only a portion of the executive group, and the new messages were to be more basic and far-reaching. The Learning group grasped the opportunity to leverage that experience, but a great gap remained. How could these busy executives, toughened by the turnaround environment, unfamiliar with learning as a business strategy, accustomed to passing communications level by level, be expected to answer Ryan's call?

Early in 1998, Ryan moved to induce learning and growth among his top two levels of management to get them into shape for the challenge. In April, he cut the ribbon on the new learning center, a landmark residential facility in Norwalk, Connecticut, and pulled in his top team for a two-day business lesson with fifty of the firm's best associates. In a sharp departure from tradition, all of the fifty were chosen without regard to rank. Instead they were picked because they each had jobs that required them to touch customers directly. At mixed tables, Prudential's top tier swapped facts, experiences and views of the future with claims adjusters, sales managers and call center operators. The occasion was wrapped in symbolism; at no time had direct dialogue taken place across Prudential's hierarchy on such a scale.

But there was also a practical matter at hand. This was the test drive for the new "learning maps," laboriously crafted tribrids of pictorial, business graph and game board produced with the ingenious Root Learning Corporation. The stakes were high; once approved, the maps were to be used in similar table sessions for every associate in the company. As learning tools, they had to be close to perfect. All the essentials of the firm's emerging competitive realities, its implied business models and its inner financial causeways had to be crammed into three table-sized maps, and the insights teased out in a fun and memorable way.

Moreover, all of us understood that the company could not tolerate a "flavor of the month exercise" —not in a turnaround, not on the brink of public ownership, not in a company in need of flexibility and speed. With the challenge of creating business literacy throughout the organization came the necessity of providing an enduring

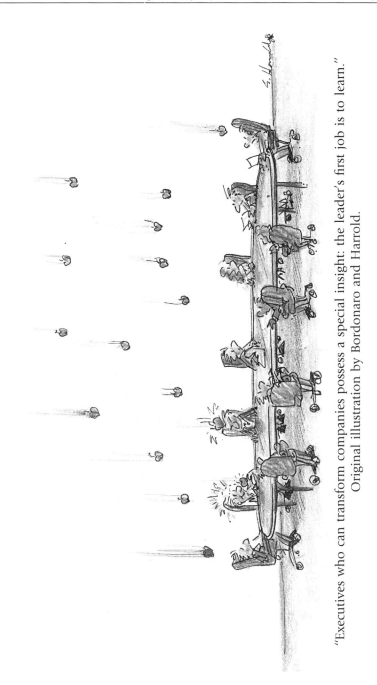

"Executives who can transform companies possess a special insight: the leader's first job is to learn."
Original illustration by Bordonaro and Harrold.

platform for learning, communication and local action across the company.

What We Did

The basics of our plan are explained in this internal document, produced by Learning project leader, Jody Doele:

"We dubbed our effort One Prudential Exchange (OPX), created a project team, and then pulled together seven sub-teams to work under it. After developing our core strategy, each sub-team submitted a complete project plan to the core team, resulting in a $38 million fully-loaded budget for the program. The sub-teams met regularly to discuss progress, identify risks and make decisions. The overall strategy was to cascade the program throughout the organization from the top down. In this way, executives and mid-level managers could become partners in teaching associates as we moved through the organization. The plan started with a one-day Leadership Launch with the top 150 executives in the company to gain their commitment and buy-in to the program. From there, Manager Meetings for ~5,000 middle level managers would be held and then ~190 Community Meetings for all associates throughout the company. Lastly, work unit meetings were held at the local level to align local work with company imperatives.

As discussed, our main objective for these initial round meetings was **business literacy**. This was accomplished mainly through the learning maps, but also from dialogue with colleagues at the tables and with executives leading the meetings. The rest of the meeting was designed to invite employees to share successes, challenges and business issues with each other (establishing an enterprise-wide platform for dialogue) and to foster a sense of "we're all in this together" across the organization.

Finally, the meetings were designed to renew a sense of local accountability in our associates. When issues were surfaced during meetings, associates were not allowed to point them out without a solution for pieces that they could control. One of our main meeting design criteria was that in each of these sessions, employees from all areas of the company would be mixed together. This helped us make strides against one of our longer-term goals—to help us destroy "silos," build community, partner, and communicate across the organization.

A second critical design criterion was that learners in one meeting became teachers and coaches in subsequent meetings. This was an opportunity for us to expand the Leadership platform, develop our leadership and management team and allow associates to interact with senior executives. To accomplish these secondary objectives, executives led all of the OPX meetings and managers were coaches at Community Meetings and leaders of work unit meetings at the local level.

All of the project materials and communication pieces were created in tandem with the OPX communication team and Prudential's internal advertising group. We created our own "logo," intranet site, numerous posters, articles, letters from the Chairman and award-winning videos to build excitement and clarity around the program across Prudential.

For a project the size of OPX, the implementation challenges were significant. One of the first major execution challenges was managing the sheer process of getting every domestic employee to a meeting. Our Meeting Management team took the lead in all of the work required to make this happen: building a 225-meeting calendar, negotiating with hotels, inviting participants and tracking attendance, travel and hotel reservations, transportation and on-site delivery of the meeting materials, and all of the A/V food and beverage and other meeting arrangements. The meeting team replaced a cumbersome e-mail /fax and memo process, which was inundating the staff and placing the project at risk. The new system saved time and money, and later became a portable asset in general use for company meetings.

After participating in the inaugural session, Art Ryan and his top 150 senior leaders maintained active involvement. Ryan joined all Manager and Community Meetings through a video in which he articulated his business strategy and commitment to OPX. Two executives from different Prudential businesses led each session. Similarly, the 4,700 middle managers who attended Manager Meetings served as table coaches at the Community Meetings, building on their leadership development. To aid in stimulating discussion and dialogue between participants, two facilitators joined the otherwise internal team running each large-scale meeting.

Work Unit Meetings were run by work unit leaders. These work unit leaders received OPX materials necessary for the meeting and then scheduled and led their Work Unit Meetings on their own."

This massive cascade became the engine and reference point for Prudential's overall learning push. For our executives, involvement was an "unavoidable opportunity" to both learn and lead. Anyone in the company's top two tiers since 1998 can tell you that they had to make a progression from learner to leader, and that the two roles overlapped, often to an uncomfortable degree. We made some suggestions to the Chairman about getting his top two levels in better condition to lead change.

Executives, Front and Center

In spring 1998, coincident with the startup of the company-wide learning, Ryan had announced a new forum for his top executives. His purposes were to provide mutual access between himself and the critical mass of leaders, to promote cross-company collaborations through discovery of common interests and build leadership skills by sharing information pulled out of the larger organization. As an antidote to the suspicions that "this too shall pass," he announced it as a leadership series and booked the first three meetings in the announcement.

Here, it may be useful to mention one of the common features of large-scale change: In almost all cases, the interweaving and mutual support of learning efforts is a matter of on-the-spot improvisation rather than meticulous planning and brilliant anticipation. The tidiness of these interweavings is sometimes surprising (remarkable?) in the rear-view mirror, and provides lots of opportunities for self-delusion and overestimation of the prophetic powers for those in-volved.

It is more truthful to state that "we knew we had to get the seniors involved in learning, we knew Art Ryan wanted a forum for reaching his leadership, and we wanted bold and inclusive learning through-out the organization." To handle the heavy traffic, we had no choice but to recruit our own management into the learning/leading for-mat, and we had a next generation of leaders to prepare, our man-agers hadn't had enough skill-building, and we had one shot to make a lot happen in very little time. Our learning team deserves a lot of credit for gutsy and clever improvisation. Under pressure, they seized emerging threads and tied them together, usually well, and often "just in time."

We devoted the July 1998 meeting to One Prudential Exchange, giving the two levels below Ryan maps 1 and 2 in the same presen-tation we expected to use with the entire organization. Although the group made several practical suggestions about the learning content and flow, it is notable that the basic delivery and supporting tools were as serviceable at these senior levels as they had been in our focus group testing. In the ensuing months, through dozens of large-scale meetings, we reaped gains in political support from those same seniors on the strength of their having "been there" through a full-length, full-strength learning program.

A second piece of July 1998 business was to obtain commitments from the participants to co-lead future meetings with mixed groups at pre-set dates and U.S. sites. A detail telling of our approach to "volunteerism": in the afternoon session, we posted out-sized sign-up sheets on the meeting room walls and invited them to swarm, mingle and slot. They did so, creating an atmosphere of jockeying-cum-networking and filling our subscription within fifteen minutes. This mood of instant commitment and acting in the moment was good for us all. It demonstrated a kind of nimbleness we would need at the new Prudential—and it may be considered a prize of acting boldly; making appointments through executive assistants is just not what it used to be. (However, the learning mind shudders to think where we would be had our morning session fallen flat.)

The leadership series was sustained having evolved into a dinner/stayover/next-day session, held twice yearly at the Center for Learning and Innovation. To a great extent, the Series reflects one chairman's style and priorities for leadership, and this evolution is a story in itself. However, the meetings have consistently supported the life and continuance of the "exchange," in its original and succeeding versions.

Just in Time

So, the leaders of Prudential spoke and listened. Vulnerable before associates of all levels and from all corners, they made learning possible and withstood the questions that arose from learning. In the liberating air of a fact-filled room, questions were fired off and fielded. Executives grow rapidly in such an environment; rapid evolution and constant readjustments are the norm.

Most often, pre-assembly breakfasts, breaks and lunch periods were occasions for fast-paced invention and decision-making, with the paired executives taking instant accountability for coverage and handling of unique meeting needs ("We've had two good questions about the Institution's new business strategy—we've got to address it in the post-Map 3 Q&A. Who's closest to this one—can we make a quick call to the planning unit and get any more info on the new market data? Which one of us should handle these questions about the New Jersey Regulator's latest reaction to our confidential filing for demutualization?" —and on and on).

How different this live action exposure is to an executive who has grown accustomed to the prepared speech within one's own business or function, the cloistered staff huddle in the familiar conference room, the carefully scripted broadcast and the polished memo! Many of our top people grew like forced bulbs. New friendships formed between partners, and many have continued consulting one another on issues of leadership.

The mixed sensations of freefall and flight are familiar to anyone who has helped lead a transformation. Substantial gains were achieved only through a combination of good planning and the self-confidence to ad lib enhancements based on immediate learnings. Besides talent and resources, three ingredients seem to have been particularly useful: a format for continual face-to-face meetings at the top of the company, abundant and continuous feedback and our adherence to a list of clear and simple design principles.

Feedback, Feedback, Feedback

Once the program was unleashed, there was great curiosity throughout the leadership ranks—how would people react? What would they do? What would they want? The learning team made a religion of obtaining feedback. We sought it from every avenue we could think of. Post-meeting questionnaires were standard. Check-in and quality check sessions were held by our facilitators and executives at breaks and at the ends of all meetings. We incorporated questions about the learning efforts into our quarterly employee attitude surveys. We retooled the survey analysis and examined key measures before and after people had gone to our sessions, calculating changes for statistical significance. We assigned roving observers to meetings and debriefed them regularly. We were on the phone constantly with executives and managers, probing for reactions and suggestions. Cornering and chatting with all manner of participants, session leaders and facilitators became a reflexive habit.

In the case of work unit meetings, which were held back on the job, we called 100 work unit leaders and obtained a binder's worth of data and perceptions on the practical application of tools and concepts. Changes made deep within the company were captured and catalogued.

Reaction to real-time feedback became part of the working style, and often meeting formats and presentations were reworked in the minutes prior to "air time." Daring to make changes was made easier by the strength of prior preparation and the virtues of repetition. It was easier to stray slightly from a well-known routine. Finally, the company's performance against key financials was tracked concurrently with the learning feedback. A quick summary of the results follows.

Level 1

- **Key Questions**: Did the participants find the learning experience engaging, interesting, relevant and useful?
- **Source**: (mainly) Post-session evaluations/table coach feedback.
- **Results**:
    1. Participants thought the session was valuable (93% favorable).
    2. Participants were clearer about the challenges facing Prudential in the financial services industry (83% favorable).
    3. Participants were engaged and excited about the Maps, and found them an excellent learning tool (table coach feedback). All key survey measures 85% or better.

Level 2

- **Key Questions**: Did the participants experience an increase in business literacy and understanding of their roles on the job?
- **Source**: (mainly) Selected items from company opinion survey.
- **Results**:
    1. Participants more clearly understood how Prudential earns and spends its money (84% favorable).
    2. Participants were committed to "doing my part" to help Prudential reach its objectives (90% favorable).
    3. Participants more clearly understand what Prudential is doing to meet the challenge of the marketplace (71% favorable).

4. Work unit's plans are in greater alignment with Prudential's strategic goals (68% favorable).

5. Participants were clear about the role they must play to implement change in their work unit (74% favorable).

Level 3

- **Key Questions**: Did the learning experience lead/contribute to actions or changes known to increase business performance?

- **Source(s)**: (1) Special "employee commitment" subscale of employee opinion survey statistically linked to customer satisfaction; and (2) Phone and in-person interview/audits of 100 work-unit meeting leaders after using Map 5 and tools locally.

- **Results**:

   1. Managers who participated in all components of OPX reported significantly higher Overall Satisfaction with the company (+8%) and a greater sense of connection to the Prudential Mission (4 questions, average of +15%).

   2. Associates who participated in all components of OPX reported significantly higher Overall Satisfaction with the company (+4%) and a greater sense of connection to the Prudential Mission (4 questions, average of +11%).

   3. Interview/audits of 100 work unit meeting leaders and action plans indicated that 37% focused on increasing efficiencies (work flows, reducing expenses), 27% involved improving technology and service (improving customer service, technology enhancements) and 23% centered on improving management and leadership (work environment, improving morale).

Level 4

- **Key Questions:** Did the business performance improve over the period of the learning effort? Are these improvements driven by secondary factors that are logically linked to performance improvements on the job?

- **Source**: Internal quarterly reports during 1997–1999.
- **Results**:
  1. Results for the 1998–2001 period included substantial increases in profitability and ROI. Corporate expenses were significantly reduced. Broad financial results always have multiple causes. The company's financial improvement is a well–known story in the investment community and coincided with the learning strategy.

  2. Retention of employees, a critical expense item, improved in direct correspondence to exposure to the new learning. Significant year-to-year increases in retention were realized over the three core years of the OPX rollout. The upward trend continued during the work unit phases that followed, and are considered a stable improvement traceable to the learning strategy.

The Principle of the Thing

Can learning successes be "bottled" and reused from company to company? That's a common question, and for good reason. Major strategic initiatives are expensive and risky. The Prudential rollout for business literacy cost about $800 per person. Executive time and organization capacity used to support the learning, and the opportunity cost of this multi-year process add up to major stakes. Being a fast follower might be a lot more comfortable, but is imitation possible?

The bad news is that, in the particulars, massive learning strategies are not repeatable. By their nature, they are woven into, and responsive to non-recurring conditions within the business. In addition, the realm of learning tools and methods evolves rapidly. Learning solutions that were more or less new to the world had to be made up to fit our immediate purpose. Other aspects, such as the learning maps, and our heavy reliance on face-to-face meetings have already evolved. Root Learning now offers desktop-distributable tools as well as physical maps, and Prudential is abuzz with technology-driven virtual communications. It helps to have done the work, but the particulars are best addressed with a blank sheet.

Fortunately, there is a major dividend from hard-won learning experience that can make the task less daunting. There are a few guidelines that are viable over a lot of situations and consistently increase the quality of learning and the company's return. They're offered here as the learning "principles." They were used rigorously in putting together the Prudential strategy. Each principle is defined below, along with an assessment of the Pru case.

Principle #1: Top Down

What it means: Learning professionals at Prudential take an implied oath that they will not ask people in the organization to learn what the most senior people have not. Hence the early Map sessions, the participation by Ryan's top two levels in leading meetings, in Next Generation training and in other initiatives that have been taken.

How we did: Achieved

You can tell almost everything about the operation of this principle by watching what the CEO did. You may recall the very first map session with "customer touching" employees. At that session, our chairman's table mates were mostly call center operators and sales reps who worked far from the corporate office. Art Ryan took notes. You can't beat that.

What was challenging about getting seniors to learn, besides the obvious, reflexive executive resistance to sitting still in a classroom? Mainly, it is the robustness of content and the medium—its ability to capture attention quickly and hold it. Here, the Root Learning maps held up extremely well through levels, starting at the top. It helped also that several leaders were involved in creating the map content.

Materials developed later for local business unit application presented some difficulty at senior levels (probably because senior jobs are not "local" but broad). Once a few of the most respected executives stepped forward, the charge that "every executive is expected to learn and help others learn" gained force. And our mania for rapid feedback cycles, speedy revision, the flexibility of staff and the extensive use of focus groups/pilot sessions played well to our high achievers.

Principle #2: Teaming at the Top

What it means: In the transforming organization, the pressures for integration are so great as to make any "star system" for developing people seem quaint. For learning efforts to matter, they must instill (even inspire) good partnering by individuals and provide options for structuring the appropriate interdependencies into the work itself. The question for learning is whether its welter of learning "productions," taken together, is causing this to take place.

How we did: Partially Achieved

Teaming was profound between the pairs of executives hosting the map sessions, and between them and their meeting facilitators and table coaches. We have described the charged atmosphere these sessions presented. It is not an exaggeration to say that co-hosting experiences fostered some enduring on-the-job partnerships. People who have done this together have often continued to keep in touch, and have volunteered for other tasks together.

A breakthrough occurred about thirty days into the large-scale meeting schedule. Executives arranged conference calls to exchange their learnings and provide tips to those who had sessions coming up. Creation of a network for the explicit purpose of lateral transfer of experience, and with no prompting or participation by professional staff, ranks high on the "signs that things are happening" list and is sure evidence of teamwork.

Still, on a day-to-day basis, the company has moved only incrementally from its "confederacy of independent units" model.

Integration has begun in earnest of late, but it is more strongly driven by shifts in business focus that require it, than by any spell cast through learning.

Prudential's "Next Generation" learning, (which includes our top 500 positions and was completed in Summer 2000), devotes a full one-third of content to "working together in the right way."

Principle #3: Inside Out

What it means: We say that, to be memorable and useful, material has to not only make sense, but matter. Behind every well-learned technique or tool is a message about its potential to move the learner closer to a desired value or goal. Thus, the learning map session is not merely a clever conveyance of knowledge, it is an enactment of values for involvement and against preaching, for discovery and against spoon-feeding, for the exchange of perceptions and against the "lone genius" system, for alignment with facts and against acceptance of "the word from management" for the leader as co-learner and example-setter and against the leader as the pretender to infallibility. Likewise, open debate about our responses to external realities delivers stress fractures to industry dogma, so those taking part begin to grasp a less comfortable but more sincere view of the world.

How we did: Achieved

Cues to success on this principle come mainly from "feel." But the data are reliable, nonetheless. Most of us look into participants' faces to gauge impact, and rely on post-meeting "buzz" to tell us what a learning process has meant. By these cues, the large-scale sessions with the first three maps yielded generous confirmation that our senior executives were finding new ways to communicate.

Many had been understandably concerned about pulling out of the office for a full two days (often with travel added on) in the midst of Prudential's turnaround. And they knew they were facing associates, many of whom were agents—in our world, that's spelled "revenue producers" —who were themselves reluctant to spend unpaid time out of the marketplace.

Yet, in this new atmosphere of learning-through-interpretation, followed-by-tough-questions, most of our seniors thrived.

Principle #4: Simultaneous Knowing and Doing

What it means: Nobody has much time for pure learning in the workplace. Separating "stuff to know" from "stuff to do" also strains the connections between insight and action. More powerful is the experience that encourages action to arise concurrent with new learnings. The idea is less formal than the "Action Learning" model, but the spirit is the same. To live this principle well, we tried to bring the points of decision as close as we could to the learning, in time and place, with minimum sacrifice of other principles.

How we did: Partially Achieved

Because of our decision to have mixed groups and deploy by geography rather than business group, table discussants could not readily employ what they had absorbed. However, certain features counterbalanced this issue. The learning tools (maps and materials) were both storable and portable, allowing local applications to take place with minimum "re-ramping." The schedule was compressed so that most local action follow-up meetings (our "work unit meetings") occurred 10–40 days after the large-scale sessions. And the leadership sessions that Art Ryan held at the start-up included immediate sign-ups and commitments in the meeting and time to discuss and resolve many logistical and process questions. Finally, the delivery style, as discussed, featured lots of huddle-and-change periods throughout.

Principle #5: Simultaneity

What it means: First used by strategy guru Ram Charan, this is the notion that organizations have to move on many fronts all at once, with spontaneity, so that the moment-to-moment content cannot be predicted. This is only possible when the organization is saturated with common language and common tools, and is thereby in readiness. Our plain aim is to get a lot of people on the same page quickly, creating learning "brands" out of visuals and tools.

How we did: The company was drenched in One Prudential Exchange. Two measures of simultaneity are: (1) How quickly were we able to work through levels? and (2) How quickly did we expose the full organization? On the first issue, the period from the first executive session to the first community meeting was about two weeks. On the second, the company-wide community meetings themselves took about fourteen months. Because our design favored mixed-unit groups, unit-to-unit timing differences were eliminated. We worked through each part of the company at the same speed. Within fourteen months of our first session, virtually all associates (96%) had experienced a large-scale learning session and a local session with teammates where on-the-job applications were discussed. Put another way, the average Prudential employee spent three to four days in session within about a one-year period.

Did simultaneity provide spontaneous application to emerging issues? Our Level 3 measures say so, as does the all-telling corporate reputation of OPX among associates at all levels.

More can be said about the importance of simultaneous learning for keeping the organization on the subject and at the task. Concentration in time can produce concentration on the "signal" in a semi-chaotic corporate workplace.

Achieving "Big Mo"

Momentum is an expected benefit of large-scale learning. As a critical mass (say 30%) of the population participates in a common experience with a shared verbal and visual language, the improvements of all parts are generated by the population itself, and the support for further learning becomes progressively easier. Our experience bore this out.

As associates returned to the workplace, small duplicates of the learning maps showed up in common work areas and on computer screens. New language for previously unclear ideas seeped into the day-to-day language. As a result, those who had not participated looked forward to it, and most saw it as a way to enhance their own effectiveness.

At senior levels, where most of the responsibility for hosting and coaching lay, support activities began to spring up, commonly in the form of teleconferences with twenty to forty executives relating recent meeting experiences, passing along tips and techniques, sharing documents and stimulating some friendly competition. We, in Learning, quickly got the idea to organize and stage these calls, but the spontaneous nature of the first few were an encouraging surprise and, looking back, a sure signal that momentum had been achieved and that learning and leading were occurring without direct supervision or control.

The Costs of Success—A Caution to Executives

On many occasions during the latter stages of our first company-wide blitz—feedback from the sessions showed an intriguing mix of compliments and complaints. People generally liked the meetings very much; they were excited about the new learnings; they credited our executives for being accessible. However, they were often sharply critical of the company's weak and incomplete communication, especially from the senior levels outward toward the customer.

Having seen a picture more close in completeness to that enjoyed in the top ranks, they had quickly acquired a taste for better, more complete, timelier information. If these were the competitive realities, how can we get more information about the competition?

If we need greater returns on our investments, what parts of our business drive this? How does my unit fit in? How can I track progress? If the markets for financial services are shifting, what decisions are our leaders making now that will assure the company winning positions in these markets? For anyone trying to manage change, the ground had shifted. The good news was that we had a well-informed population; and the challenge was that we had a well-informed population. Insight had brought on the demand for information, and our leaders were on the hook for it.

Large learning efforts like this one are becoming part of the big company transformation repertoire. Done well, and with adherence to the right principles, they become distinctive in the minds of participants, yet indistinguishable from the firm's overall strategic, operational and financial efforts. They become the language and structure of change. They impart hope, excitement and, at best, a resolve to win.

Yet, they bring with them a fearsome backlash of expectations and future work, as a more knowing organization demands a constant flow of better information from top management, clearer direction from middle management, and, everywhere, local action that responds directly to these messages. That is why, at Prudential, our executives now work constantly to become the better leaders we taught our people they deserve. Being good at learning raises the bar.

And the bar, once reset, tends to resist retreat. On March 29, 2000 Pru's executive in charge of our finance function and demutualization effort explained to our top 150 executives: "Although reduced expenses is a key to our success in the public markets, we will continue to invest in people development at above-benchmark levels, because we believe it helps us do the other things well." Let the record show that Prudential Financial in the final phases of its "coming out" as a public company, fully expecting to be pressed by investors to be quick with the blade, declared a place for learning in the newer, leaner reality.

Epilogue

During 2002, the company has simplified its corporate structure, continued to trim expenses and reduced the corporate-driven dollars spent on learning. Having achieved "launch," the firm is now more selective in its learning investments, preferring smaller-gauged efforts, closer to the business. Tighter links to "real-time" business building projects get preference.

Under Art Ryan, the Chairman's meetings continue, as does the preparation of next generation executives. Fittingly, the new corporate learning investments dwell less on "business literacy" and more on "how we run the company." Now that priorities are well understood and Prudential's new face is clear to see, the firm is paying rigorous attention to roles, responsibilities and execution of strategy. They are doing so with a deepened confidence as leaders, and with the learning principles firmly in hand.

This chapter was contributed by Dr. Frank P. Bordonaro, Chief Learning Officer of Prudential from 1997 to early 2002. F rank now acts as an independent consultant to organizations on the subjects of learning strategy, executive development and change.

CHAPTER 9

A Comprehensive Approach to Organizational Learning: Total Learning Architecture

Overview

A new and innovative approach to learning in any organization has been named *Total Learning Architecture*™ by its creator, Dr. Warren Wilhelm of the Global Consulting Alliance (GCA).

The basic premise of TLA is that all members of an organization need to learn about a core of information and skills important to the organization's success; but that people at different organizational levels need to learn about these core components to a greater or lesser extent depending on the particular subject or skill. A TLA provides for the necessary learning to the degree and in the form most relevant for each organizational member.

Building a Total Learning Architecture

Creating a TLA may be relatively straightforward, or it may be a more complex undertaking. It is unique to each organization that creates one. There are several different contextual factors that must be considered when creating a TLA.

Competitive Strategy

Utilizing concepts taken from Treacy and Wirkzema's *Discipline of Market Leaders*, organizations can differentiate themselves in three different ways. First, those who wish to compete based on "operational excellence," that is, low price, will require virtuosity in one set of skills, knowledge and behaviors to excel in that niche. Second, those who differentiate themselves on "technological innovation" will require emphasis on a different set of skills. Finally, those who compete based on "customer intimacy" will require yet another set.

Existing Leadership and Management Development Processes

Every organization has some form of leadership and management development process already in place. These processes include both formal and informal learning processes and coaching. They also include learning that is delivered internally and externally to the organization. It is critical that these processes be acknowledged, understood and factored into a TLA.

Organizations have varying degrees of investment in their existing leadership and management development processes. One organization may not want anything "thrown away" in the new TLA. They prefer that any new learning processes be built explicitly on the foundation that already exists within their organization. In another company, the exact opposite may hold true. The company leadership may feel that the organization "needs something different" and will insist that new programs look and sound very different from their predecessors.

Measurement Processes

Organizations have varying ways of measuring the efficiency and effectiveness of their leadership/management development processes including: (1) anecdotal measures; (2) "smile sheets," which ask how satisfied participants were with the program and how well they liked it; (3) measures of comprehension; (4) measures of behavioral change; (5) correlations with the financial bottom line of the organization; and (6) intangible benefits; returns on the investment made in the learning that cannot be quantified, but are perceived as valuable. For example, "We promised that every employee would be offered the opportunity to grow professionally, and we've followed through on that promise."

Another set of measurement criteria is often referred to as the "butts in seats" set of measures. Many organizations pay attention to the number of classes conducted, the number of training hours per employee, the ratio of students per instructor and the percentage change (usually increase) in these measures over time.

Each of these measurement processes indicates a different level of organizational sophistication and maturity. As the TLA is developed, an organization's existing measures—and its capacity to change—must be taken into account.

A different perspective on measurement processes comes from an evaluation of how the organization pays for its learning programs. Is the training and development (T&D) function a cost center or a profit center? Are training costs allocated evenly across the organization, allocated on a proportional basis or allocated based on actual usage? Is the T&D function the "sole supplier" of training, or do they compete with other internal or external suppliers? The answer to these questions plays a major role in determining the amount of resources that may be available for the development of a TLA.

Training Infrastructure, Communication and Information Processing Processes

Organizational infrastructures vary widely. Some organizations have a centralized training and development structure, while others embed it within decentralized business units. Some have separate vice presidents in each area while others only have one. In most cases, these functions report to the senior vice president in charge of human resources.

Some organizations utilize their Local Area Networks (LANs), Wide Area Networks (WANs) and company intranets to provide information regarding their program offerings, facilitate registration and scheduling, and track T&D statistics. Others use manual, paper-and-pencil approaches.

Each of these arrangements impacts the design and implementation of a TLA. Centralized, powerful T&D functions have the advantage of consistency, yet may not be finely tuned to the needs of the workforce. Decentralized functions are typically very attuned to the needs of their particular employees, yet may vary widely in their product and service offerings.

High tech organizations are able to take advantage of their (virtually) free ability to communicate to employees to provide a tremendous amount of information. The downside of this approach can be a tendency to "tell everyone everything," which is a way to greatly increase the chance that important information will be buried under a mountain of interesting, yet non-essential messages. The opposite is true for organizations that focus mainly on word-of-mouth/bulletin board/memo types of communications.

Learning Culture

Organizations place differing values on learning. In some, it is best characterized as an "item to get checked off the list." In others, it is considered "something to be done (if and when) money and time permit." These are the types of organizations that at the first sign of financial downturn identify the T&D department as one of the first budgets to be cut. Yet others consider training as a reward—a boon-doggle; an opportunity to take some time out of the office, often at a nice resort, where golf is an essential element of the learning program.

There are, of course, organizations for which learning is perceived as an essential source of competitive advantage. These organizations usually take the stance that their people are the only asset that cannot be replicated and that (with the proper attention) will not become obsolete. This type of company usually recognizes that offering their employees opportunities for professional and personal growth is a powerful motivator, one that engenders creativity, innovation and loyalty.

With awareness of the organization's existing leadership and management development processes, measurement processes, training infrastructure, communication and information processing processes, and learning culture, the formulation of a Total Learning Architecture can begin.

Training versus Learning

The TLA concept recognizes the distinctions between "training" and "learning"; the difference between attending a class and putting the skills learned in that class to use in daily work (and away-from-work) behavior. In an organization with a "one size fits all" training structure, management assumes that: (1) there are universal skills that are needed by everyone, so why not train them all; (2) even if they already know it, a review "could not hurt"; and (3) full classes produce a great instructor/student ratio.

Adult learning theory and past experience suggest that these assumptions do not serve organizations well. They fail to take into consideration the "opportunity cost" of participants' time; that is, the perceived value of what else they might have been doing if they were not attending the training class. If a busy manager feels that s/he could have been in their office making decisions that would have provided significant benefit to the organization, s/he will feel resentful if the training is not perceived as providing at least that much immediate or future "return on time invested."

The one size fits all assumption also does not take into account the principles of adult learning theory that suggest that adults learn best when they have an immediate need for the knowledge, and an immediate opportunity to put that knowledge into use. Asking a busy professional to attend a class that they feel is irrelevant, "beneath them" or that they will not use immediately is likely to induce resentment, indifference and no change in behavior at the conclusion of the training.

In organizations where the concept of learning as opposed to training has taken hold, employees actively search out the learning experiences they need when a specific opportunity is identified. Recognizing that the learning experience could take many forms (classroom training, self-paced learning, a conversation with another employee, reading an article, etc.), employees proactively identify the choices available to them and select one based on what will provide the greatest return for the time they will invest in gaining the learning.

Their manager, who also has a vested interest in the employee acquiring the new skill, is an active partner in the learning process and provides support and feedback. This could take the form of "checking in" with the employee to see how things are going, being available to answer questions, and providing support and encouragement as the employee struggles through the challenges of putting new learning into practice.

Recognizing the nuances between the philosophies and dynamics of a learning organization and a training organization helps pave the way for a discussion of the three phases of a TLA framework.

Three Phases of a Total Learning Architecture

There are three phases in a TLA: (1) inputs; (2) delivery vehicles; and (3) learning locks. These three components comprise a learning process (as opposed to a training event); all three phases are essential to maximize an employee's learning experience.

Phase 1

The first phase of the framework begins with the concept of **inputs**. Inputs are the processes already in place, or that must be created, to assure that the right people are getting the right learning opportunities at the right time. Inputs can take a variety of different forms as shown in Figure 1.

Vision and values. The organization's vision and values provide insights about the kinds of knowledge, behaviors and skills that are essential for the organization to be successful. If the organization claims that "Quality is Job 1," then it is a safe bet that everyone in the organization must learn about quality. Likewise, if one of the organization's stated values is, "We value the contributions of every individual," then explicit learning and focus on diversity is needed for that value to be operationalized within the organization.

Needs assessment. A comprehensive assessment of the learning needs of an organization provides another input to the TLA. This is accomplished by a combination of surveys (either paper-and-pencil

Figure 1:   Total Learning Architecture—The Three Phases

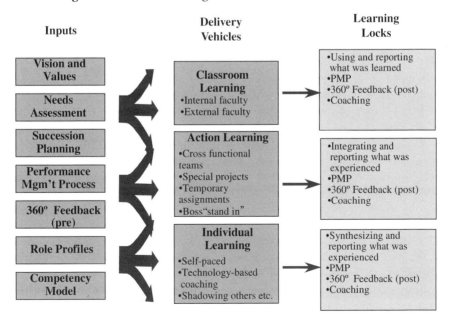

or computer-based), personal interviews and assessment of the organization's competitive environment. The primary learning needs, identified using this methodology, become the core of the TLA.

Succession planning. Succession planning identifies individuals within the organization who are perceived as having the ability to populate positions of leadership, either immediately or at some point in the future. Based on that determination, it is possible to identify the knowledge, skills and behaviors they must learn in order to be successful in their current and future positions.

Performance management process. This process often contains a developmental component. Whether to bolster weak areas or leverage strengths, well designed performance reviews identify specific areas that employees need to focus on before the next performance management process review (usually a year).

360° Feedback. These processes (also called multi-rater feedback processes) provide confidential, candid feedback on the participant's strengths and opportunities for development from a variety of perspectives. Typically managers, peers and direct inputs are compared to the person's own self-assessment to provide a "holographic" picture around the specific items and scales identified during the design of the 360° instrument. These data often provide individuals with a powerful incentive for change.

Role profiles. Such profiles, often derived from **competency models**, provide another way of focusing attention on particular skills, knowledge and behaviors. Industry associations, professional groups and consulting firms often generate profiles of characteristics of the "best in class" organizations in particular areas. As an example, the Association for Quality and Participation has identified twelve Key Skills Areas for facilitators; and Global Consulting Alliance, in partnership with the University of Michigan, has developed a Human Resources Competency Model. These models allow organizations, teams and individuals to benchmark their own abilities against competitive norms. This benchmarking process may identify developmental areas not immediately obvious based on the organization's own current processes or performance.

In a TLA, a series of discussions and investigations identifies which of these processes are already in place, and which need to be modified or created. Taken together, they will maximize the chance that participants in any learning situation will perceive a need for that learning, have an opportunity to exploit it and will realize a positive return on time invested for their learning investment.

Phase 2

The second phase of the TLA concentrates on identifying and providing the appropriate **delivery vehicles** to provide the needed learning programs. A traditional T&D model utilizes formal, instructor-led, classroom-style environments as the primary—and in many cases only—training delivery vehicle. This is by no means the only way of conveying learning, however, and the TLA initiates review of a broader set of options. Some of those options are shown in Figure 1.

Classroom learning. This type of learning can be a powerful delivery vehicle when used appropriately in certain situations. Questions to be asked include: Do the workshops feature primarily one-way ("I tell, you listen") or two-way ("I ask, you respond") communication? Do they use only media (e.g., overhead projection) or multiple media? Are they one-hour sessions, or four-week, offsite residential programs?

Action learning. In some situations, learning by doing is the best way to learn. Someone interested in learning to ride a bicycle can read books, watch the videos and listen to professional bike riders, yet they will still stumble and fall when they first get on the bicycle. Recognizing this, certain skills are best learned through assignments that encourage (force) participants to use the skills they need to master. A powerful way to learn to collaborate effectively is to put a group of people into a situation where they must partner effectively in order to accomplish their task.

Individual learning. This type of learning is becoming increasingly powerful and affordable. Authoring languages allow organizations to develop computer-based, self-paced learning programs internally, without the massive time and dollar expenditures that characterized early efforts. Local Area Networks (LANs), corporate intranets and CD-ROMs make it easy to share the large files that are needed to provide quality learning programs.

Distance learning. Distance learning is also based on advances in technology. This type of delivery vehicle allows a subject matter expert (SME) in one place to broadcast his or her ideas via satellite, phone line, or streaming audio and video to any number of sites worldwide. Certain technologies allow the presenter to get real time feedback in the way of return video feeds, email or "interactive relay chat" (IRC).

Neuro-Linguistic Programming. A branch of psychology, NLP emphasizes that people can learn and change by "modeling" or "shadowing" the thoughts and behaviors of others. Seeing a professional golfer make a "perfect" golf swing helps ingrain those behaviors into the viewer. Hearing what the pro golfer says to him or herself, feeling what the pro feels, seeing what the pro sees are all ways that someone can model another in order to "pick up their good habits." The same thing holds true for learning better management and leadership behaviors. Shadowing a role model, participating in cross-functional teams and temporary projects, and rotating job assignments are all ways this "learn by doing" delivery vehicle can be operationalized.

Each delivery vehicle requires another set of decisions about who will design and deliver the learning programs. Will they be developed and/or taught by internal SMEs or external academics, consultants or SMEs? Each has its own benefits and offsetting concerns. External sources can provide high levels of expertise, a larger amount of resources and greater focus (the client's job is often the only one they have). When the engagement is finished, external sources can be released without penalty. On the downside, external sources may also be more expensive, and they will take their learning from the project and may apply it to others.

Internal sources often have the opposite set of benefits and concerns. They are usually less expensive to utilize (even with burden cost—the opportunity cost of their time is sometimes a factor), and the knowledge they gain as a result of their work remains inside the organization. On the other hand, many internal people have not been trained in instructional design, training delivery or coaching. As a result, it is realistic to expect longer development times and a lower quality of the initial learning programs as the internal program developers go through their own learning curve.

Phase 3

Many organizations assume that with the proper use of input channels to provide the right training to the right people, and effective delivery of the training, that **the new skills, knowledge and behaviors will now be resident in the participants.** There are two conceptual models that explain why this is *not* usually the case.

One model, derived from adult learning theory, suggests that learners move from "unconscious incompetence" (ignorance is bliss) to "conscious incompetence" (I know I do not know, and know that I want or need to). These two stages correlate to the input stage of the TLA. The initial transfer of learning through one of the delivery vehicles moves learners to the third stage of "conscious competence" (I know I have the basics, however I am not very confident in applying them). The final stage of "unconscious competence" (I am no longer aware that I am using the new learning—I have integrated it into my behavioral and knowledge repertoire) only comes with practice.

A second model that reinforces the same points comes from Kenneth Blanchard. In his Situational Leadership II framework,

Blanchard documents the cycle from "not knowing at all, not confident," to "knowing something, but not enough to use it yet," to "knowing enough to try, but not confident," to "knowing and very confident." Leadership actions are described for each step. In the beginning of the cycle, "directing" is needed. As people begin to have questions, "coaching" is appropriate. As they begin applying the new skills in the real world, "support" is essential. Finally, as people gain experience and confidence, "delegation" frees up the leader to move on to other tasks. Blanchard discusses the risks of skipping steps along the cycle, especially the third step—assuming that people do not need support simply because they have attended formal training.

These conclusions provide support for the third phase of the TLA—**learning locks.** "Locking" the learning recognizes the need for the learning imparted via the delivery vehicles to be nurtured, reinforced, measured, recognized and rewarded. There are several ways this can take place, as shown in Figure 1.

Self-assessments provide one locking mechanism. Requesting that participants reflect at regular intervals after the formal learning on what they have tried, what worked, what did not work and what additional help is needed keeps the concepts visible to the participants.

Assessments by others provide a complementary perspective. Knowing that a coach or manager will be asked to provide feedback on progress is a powerful motivator.

A post-learning 360° assessment provides an "after" measure of change that can be compared to a pre-learning 360° assessment.

Mentoring or other support processes provide an environment where others in similar situations help each other to integrate the new learning. "Helping each other win" is the objective in the most successful of these kinds of locking processes.

The organization's **performance management process (PMP)** typically provides formal measurement of progress since the last performance appraisal. In many cases, compensation increases are integrated into the PMP, providing the "reward" component of the process.

The three phases of a TLA—inputs, delivery vehicles and learning locks—must be customized to each organization based on the organizational dimensions described in the beginning of this chapter. When designed and implemented effectively, they provide a powerful foundation for organizational learning.

Organizational Segmentation

As mentioned earlier, "one size fits all" training models overly simplify the learning requirements for most organizations. In addition to the needs for customization defined by the "inputs" phase of the TLA, three additional issues must be addressed.

One is the **need for consistency between management levels** and business units within a segment of the organization. Common sense suggests that if senior leaders learn one model of decision making, mid-level managers another and first-line supervisors a third, that there will be confusion and mistakes as the three levels interact around decision making.

The second issue focuses on **the need for consistency between segments of the organization.** Continuing the example from the previous paragraph, if the manufacturing areas learn one model of problem solving, the engineering areas another and the corporate support areas yet a third, cross-functional problem-solving teams will struggle.

The TLA framework takes these issues into consideration by assuring that appropriate levels of detail and consistency are maintained within and between the different levels and departments of the organization. Each organization needs to decide what process it will use to segment its employee population. When considering segmentation within an organizational segment, the appropriate measure may be by title, grade, tenure, skill level or the competencies needed for job success. In other companies, the Hay points grading of particular positions may be employed (see Figure 2).

Clustering Content

A third issue is that, though there needs to be consistency to assure "apples to apples" communication, **different organizational segments may need to understand the same topic in differing levels of detail.**

Business acumen, for example, is knowledge of "the business of the business." This topic is often identified by organizations as one that needs to be better understood by all employees. Different levels of employees have different learning needs within this topic area. Non-exempt employees may benefit from understanding the general concepts of profit, loss and cash flow. First-line supervisors need to understand not only those concepts, but understand the concept of managing an expense budget and dealing with budget variances. Mid-level managers add the additional requirements of budget creation and capital planning. Senior leaders often struggle with the business justification and implications of mergers and acquisitions.

Figure 2:   Levels of a Total Learning Architecture—Bands I – V

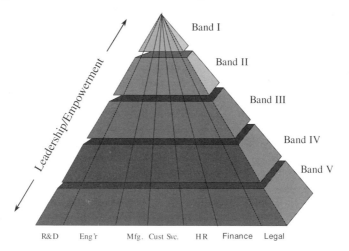

Once an organization has been divided into segments, the specific content of the learning content streams can then be identified. One of the unique aspects of the TLA is its ability to allow content segmentation to vary as appropriate for both the content and the employee groupings. For one subject (for example, the organization's vision and values), course content could be clustered into two segments—understanding the vision and values for all employees, and creating a vision and values for departmental or divisional heads. The business acumen example demonstrates a situation where the single learning program might have five content offerings given to various levels; corporate ethics might be a single learning program with one content offering given to everyone in the organization regardless of level (see Figure 3).

Dimensions of a Total Learning Architecture

Based on a detailed understanding of the organization, the three phases of the TLA, the appropriate segmentation of the organiza-

Figure 3:   Different Learning Content for Different
Organizational Levels

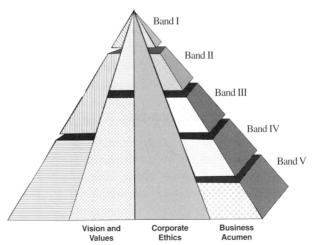

tion's employees, and the appropriate clustering of course content, it is possible to take the next step in formulating a TLA.

While this chapter will discuss each of the five dimensions individually, a TLA is best thought of as a "Rubik's Cube," a multidimensional model where each dimension interacts with the others. This concept illustrates the simultaneous nature of a TLA, and the fact that there is an almost infinite combination of factors possible (see Figure 4).

The Foundation: Existing Organizational Culture, Process and Direction

Total Learning Architectures are (virtually) never created in a vacuum. They are developed within an existing organizational context. Sometimes the context is positive—organizations that are profitable, growing and have a high regard for the HR and T&D functions. Sometimes the context is less favorable—the organization feels like

Figure 4:   The Multiple Dimensions of a Total Learning Architecture

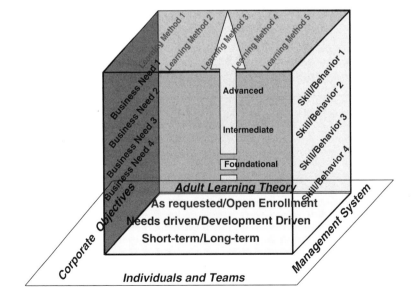

their T&D function has been, and/or is now ineffective. No matter what the case, there are always employees, often in senior leadership positions, who have a vested interest in the organization's current methodologies and processes. To ignore those feelings is to court disaster—not due to any weakness in the TLA itself, but due to predictable political resistance and sabotage.

A strategy that has proven effective when developing a TLA is to acknowledge the past, create explicit linkages to existing processes where possible and **position the TLA as an evolution rather than a revolution.** Involving those people invested in the creation of the organization's existing processes is also an effective way to manage this powerful dynamic.

The First Dimension: Business Needs

Assumption: most organizations can no longer afford to provide their workforce with "training for training's sake." They require that their learning programs be relevant, and responsive to the needs of the business. Therefore, the first dimension of the TLA is a compilation of compelling issues that the organization has addressed in the past, is currently dealing with and expects to be facing in the future. These business needs should be the ones that "keep business leaders up at night;" that have resisted early attempts to address them. These are the "critical few" business needs that could make or break the company. Developing this list of business needs can be a complex task, requiring the input of key stakeholders from within and outside the organization.

The Second Dimension: Skills and Behaviors

The focus of this dimension of the TLA is practical: **What is it that employees need to know and do more, less or differently in order to help the organization achieve its objectives?** Specifically, what are the skills or behaviors needed to improve the bottom line? This distinction means that concepts like "being a better leader" needs to be operationalized into specific behaviors. Being a better leader for one organization may be different than for another. Based on the business needs identified in the first dimension, one company may need to teach its leaders to focus more on the long-term strategic and financial implications of their decisions. Another company may need its leaders to focus more on the communication skills that enable them to clearly communicate the changes the organization needs to make in the immediate future.

One of the internal validity checks within the TLA is whether or not each of the skills and behaviors identified by the organization in the second dimension map back to at least one of the compelling business issues identified and targeted in the first dimension. If they do not, the question the organization needs to ask itself is: Is this a critical learning need? If not, the company should rethink whether that particular business need should be included, its relative priority and how it will be sourced (this item might be made available through a local university, for example).

The Third Dimension: Learning Methodologies

The three phases of the TLA—inputs, delivery vehicles and learning locks—are explicitly integrated into the third dimension. Given the specific business needs, and the skills and behaviors identified in the first two dimensions of the TLA, what is the best way to identify who needs what learning? What specific content should be made available to the various employee layers? What is the best way to deliver that content? What processes will be utilized to ensure that the learning content is supported after the formal delivery phase of the learning, and that the behaviors will be integrated into daily work behavior?

Once the critical business needs of the organization have been established, and the skills or behaviors needed to address the business needs have been determined, the next step is to decide which learning methodologies will be employed to deliver the learning. Learning methodologies employed in the third dimension are: classroom learning, distance learning, action learning, experiential learning, technology-based learning and simulations. The learning methodologies that are used depends on the type of learning being delivered, the size of the audience, the sophistication of the audience, cost allotted for the program, etc. No matter what method(s) are selected to deliver the learning, **the appropriate learning locks must be instituted and become part of the corporate climate in order for the learning to be effective.**

Unfortunately, it is far too easy for companies to creep back into their "tried and true" training and development paradigms after the formal delivery of learning if the learning locks are not instituted and nurtured, reinforced, measured, recognized and rewarded regularly. Especially for organizations who are explicitly trying to "do something different," utilizing their usual T&D methodologies often elicits negative reactions from the other employees in the organization. In this situation, comments from the workforce may include: "More of the same." "Same stuff with a different logo." "They don't 'walk their own talk.'" Therefore, it is absolutely crucial that in order for the learning to be completely successful company wide, there has to be tight integration between the learning content, the learning methodologies and the learning locks.

The Fourth Dimension: Access/Entry

Adding additional complexity to the TLA is the reality that employees enter into learning situations in a variety of different ways. These different access/entry points may best be considered as a series of scales or continuums. The following are the ways that employees access or enter learning situations. These, too, should be considered as a "Rubik's Cube," since there are a variety of combinations possible.

1. **Individual/Group:** Individuals often require new skills and behaviors; sometimes the focus is on a poorly functioning team.

2. **Urgent/Not Urgent:** When the person or team is addressing a "mission critical" or deadline-driven task, the need for new skills and behaviors may be urgent. In other situations, there may be less time pressure.

3. **Self-Initiated/Other-Initiated:** In some cases, the individual willingly seeks out new learning. In other cases, an individual or team may be "strongly urged" or told to attend. This distinction is subtle, yet makes a great deal of difference in the attitude the learner is likely to have as s/he enters the learning situation.

4. **Open Enrollment/Customized:** Depending on the content being presented and employee level, some learning may be offered to "anyone who would like to come" (e.g., time management), while others are very specialized and may be offered only to particular individuals or groups in very specific situations (e.g., a team getting ready to initiate a merger or acquisition).

The TLA must be flexible enough to accommodate each of these situations.

The Fifth Dimension: Level of Complexity

This dimension most explicitly integrates the "levels" dimension of the TLA. It recognizes that the same business need may require different skills and behaviors, learning methodologies and access/entry points depending on the level at which the issue is viewed.

This concept can be illustrated with the example of employee turnover. A first-line supervisor may be dealing with this as an urgent issue—having difficulty meeting daily production quotas. S/he might benefit from immediate help with listening, problem solving and motivation skills. A mid-level manager might require help with better understanding the business impact of turnover. Senior leaders may require new perspectives for looking at the issue in light of their vision, mission and values. What does turnover say about how well they are demonstrating their values of "people," "integrity" and "teamwork?"

A mixed-level team might need to be convened to assess the supporting information, communication, measurement, and recognition and reward systems to bring them into alignment in order to address the issue in a manner consistent with the organization's objectives.

Total Learning Architecture: Learning from Experience

Due to the number and complexity of the factors involved, the design of a TLA is not simple. Experience so far has shown that simply transporting a TLA from one organization to another is not practical—the unique context of each organization requires that it create its own.

Communication

An explicit communication strategy is key for the success of a TLA. What is a TLA? How is it different from what the organization was doing before? How do people enter the system? What is the timeframe for design and implementation? In the absence of regular communication, the organization's rumor mill will generate its own; information that is not always accurate and that can be damaging to the objectives of the new processes being introduced. Thus, it is absolutely essential that the entire organization is aware of the goals and objectives of the TLA process, and is informed of the expected outcomes.

Continuity

A TLA is best thought of as work perpetually in progress. It is very tempting to rush out a complete catalog of new learning opportunities for the organization. This usually results in poor quality, "more of the same" offerings. A relevant folk saying is, "You never get a second chance to make a first impression." It is essential that care be taken with the initial learning programs delivered under the TLA umbrella. It is far more advantageous to pilot a small number of high-quality learning programs than to succumb to organizational wishes for "everything yesterday." An effective communication plan will keep the organization informed of current offerings and the timeframe for future ones, so employees can plan accordingly.

Required Investment

Finally, creation of a TLA requires significant investment by the organization. With so many factors at work, and so many stakeholders impacted by the results (every employee), it is critical that time, expertise and input from representative samples of the organization be brought to bear on this process. Several organizations have formed a "Steering Committee" or "Advisory Council," comprised of a "diagonal slice" of the organization in order to assure that the various perspectives are represented. External experts experienced in assisting organizations through this process can also be invaluable in minimizing difficulties and increasing the speed of TLA design and implementation.

Summary

The last decades have been characterized by sweeping change in virtually every area of organizational life. New awareness about adult learning theory, instructional design, benchmarking and knowledge sharing, as well as innovations in technology have improved these respective areas in human resource management, and training and development. **The concept of Total Learning Architecture provides an integrating mechanism that synthesizes these advances to enable organizations to better meet their strategies, goals and objectives.**

This chapter was contributed by Lawrence Solow of 3-D Change, Inc., a consulting firm that specializes in organizational development, large-scale change and total quality.

CHAPTER **10**

Summary of Learning Architectures

This book has been a journey through organizational learning. We first made the case for Why Learning Matters. If, as Peter Drucker has said, an organization's ability to learn faster than its competition is the only sustainable competitive advantage, then learning capability must be infused and enhanced in successful organizations. This is, of course, easier said than done.

Some organizations have continuous learning as a part of their corporate DNA; others must acquire it as a new skill. A significant component of GE's success over time has been its ability to develop competent leaders within its own culture. Its leadership learning center, Crotonville, has allowed GE to develop perhaps the deepest leadership bench of all corporations in the U.S. Similarly, Intel has a corporate mindset that requires and supports continuous learning. Their self-described mindset of "paranoid collaboration" drives intensive learning by all employees all the time.

Other companies, like Herman Miller, have learned successfully how to infuse their organization with desired knowledge when necessity demands it. Still others have yet to learn either the competitive value of learning or how to do it on an organizational scale. Whenever it begins, the enhancement and perpetuation of systematic learning creates major competitive advantages for an organization. **This book is an attempt to help organizations of all kinds create and manage a learning architecture.**

We have looked at organizations with widely varying learning needs. Some are small and centralized; others are large and geographically dispersed. We have looked at non- and not-for-profit organizations that have missions somewhat different from stockholder-owned, for-profit companies. Some companies sell consumer goods, some are OEMs, and others sell services. Regardless of an organization's specifics, learning must be imbedded in the company's corporate DNA if it is to succeed and prosper.

Learning and Learning Structure are Important

It is unrealistic to expect that haphazard or random learning will advance an organization very far. In most companies we can find individuals who proactively seek out university courses, seminars and workshops to attend for their personal learning. This is great for the people who take the initiative, but it usually only benefits those individuals; the organization itself is rarely affected. In order to gain the benefits of learning, an organization must have a way to structure learning for all its members, and for the entire collective organization itself. This is where a learning architecture enters the picture. It represents a thoughtful approach to learning for individual members of the organization, and for the organization as a whole.

Two Approaches to Learning Structures

Learning can be structured using either inductive or deductive logic for learning structure design. Learning architectures built inductively begin with the components: individual learning, group classes, IT structures and software, and larger learning programs. These individual building blocks come together to form the total learning architecture.

Deductively built learning architectures begin with the big picture and break it down into successively smaller components. Someone, or some ones, decides on the overall purpose of the organization's learning, then constructs the various pieces necessary to make the learning a reality. Structures built deductively include: focused learning for individuals according to their personal needs, group learning directed to people who share the same learning needs, enabling technology, and other learning supports such as coaching and mentoring.

Of the two choices, inductively versus deductively built learning architectures, those built using deductive logic tend to be superior. Beginning from the big picture insures that all relevant learning needs can be addressed. It also allows all the components of the learning architecture to intersect cleanly with one another, and complement one another.

To deductively build a learning architecture, it is first necessary to inventory all the learning needs in the organization. The structure is then built to address all the learning needs at all levels. Learning architectures built deductively tend to be comprehensive and well integrated.

Learning structures that simply evolve over time, one component at a time being added, tend to be more diffuse and less efficient than deductively built structures. They usually have duplication of learning, empty spots where desirable learning does not exist, and what does exist does not work together as a whole. When a new Chief Learning Officer came to AlliedSignal in 1993, there were over 400 learning programs throughout the 90,000 employee company. For many topics, two or more programs existed to teach the same thing. One of the first tasks of the new CLO was to rationalize the learning structure by identifying the best program to teach each needed learning topic, and then to eliminate all the duplicative programs. This resulted in massive cost savings, as well as a much more effective learning architecture. As a result, employees could receive the best possible learning available on any topic. The total number of courses and topical offerings was streamlined to less than 150.

Learning Structures That Work Best

The characteristics of learning architectures that are effective and efficient are:

- They are built on a comprehensive learning needs analysis.
- They address all identified learning needs in the organization.
- Learning is integrated into the daily activities of the organization; it does not stand alone, and it is not disconnected from the organizational mission.
- They give only the required amount of learning to people at different organizational levels; they do not overteach or underteach.
- Learning at each level, and to each learner, is world class in its quality.
- Learning is just-in-time, not just-in-case.
- Speed is an important aspect of learning.
- Learning pedagogies are chosen carefully to be most effective for the intended learner(s).
- Learning at each level is integrated with learning at all other levels.
- Learners at one level teach at another level.
- Results of learning are measured with real, relevant metrics.
- Good learning architectures are cost-effective and have collective buying power.
- They are designed and administered from one central focal point (often a CLO).
- All members of the organization know what learning is available and how to access it.
- Learning has the unwavering support of the organization's leaders.
- Continuous learning is expected of all organization members.

These characteristics can serve as a checklist to assess the quality of an organization's learning architecture. Each characteristic was discussed earlier in this book. A superb learning architecture will rate high on all these characteristics.

Learning Approaches Approaching Obsolescence

Ten or fifteen years ago many if not most companies thought of learning (training, at the time) as an add-on, a nice-to-do, in many cases a 'perk' to reward deserving employees. There was often little connection between the training that was offered and the chance to put it to immediate use. Typical training lasted two or more weeks, was held at a golf resort, consisted of a parade of enjoyable speakers and included plenty of social time for the participants. This kind of training, although of dubious value to the business, generally got great smile ratings from the participants.

Alternatively, companies sent their managers and leaders off to university programs, seminars given by consultants and socially enjoyable professional meetings. Usually only one or two people from any organization would attend the same training event. Participants often welcomed the time out of the office. Sometimes these extended training programs were used to prepare a leader for a promotion to a bigger job, or even to network because they would soon need to find themselves another job. Many of these programs were very long by today's standards: the Harvard PMD (Program for Management Development) and AMP (Advanced Management Program) were as long as thirteen weeks.

These types of learning are rapidly becoming obsolete. Because of the time and competitive pressures on almost every organization, today's learning must address a clear and present learning need, be just-in-time, be focused and concise, quickly delivered and absorbed, and be demonstrably cost-effective. It is also valuable for several if not many members of the same organization to learn the same things at the same time. As a result, the best learning offered and delivered today looks a lot different from just a decade ago.

University-based Programs

Perhaps the biggest change is in the use of university-based programs. While many universities have adjusted to marketplace demand by shortening their programs, many are still seen as too long. Another problem with university-based programs is that companies can seldom send more than one or two participants to the same program at the same time, so the value-added component of many people from the same organization learning together is lost. University-based programs are also relatively expensive when compared with in-house, company-specific ones. Finally, most universities are constrained to using only their own faculty to teach in their programs. Since not all the faculty at any school is of consistently high talent, the average talent level of a university faculty is not as high as can be achieved with a "cherry-picked" faculty of the best experts available anywhere who come together in a custom program. For all these reasons, open-enrollment university-based programs are one type of learning that is no longer valued as highly as it once was.

Not sitting idly by while organizations look for different, more effective sources of learning, universities have responded to the changing learning environment by offering new approaches to their programs. Most major universities will now custom-tailor a learning program to the unique needs of a company or organization, and deliver it to large numbers of organizational members at the same time. These programs are often delivered on the school's campus, but also may be delivered on a company's own site or at another rented location.

While more responsive to the organization's learning needs, the customized university programs still suffer the fatal flaw of having to use only the university's own faculty, often inconsistent in quality. And they are expensive, because universities have large overhead burdens that must be serviced. So university programs, while they have evolved over the past decade, are often not the learning provider of choice for enlightened organizations.

Also less popular are the kind of company programs described earlier: more than a week in length, a parade of speakers, lots of social time and not urgently needed. We rarely see programs of this type anymore, at least in the U.S. In fact, the only learning that has currency today is short, quick and focused on a specific need or problem, and filled with serious content. To receive this learning, participants must have an immediate use for what they learn and be judged, by virtue of their performance, to be worthy of the investment of time and expense in their development.

Cost-Effective Learning

It has always been difficult, if not impossible, to calculate with precision the value of organizational learning. While we cannot calculate the exact return on investment from learning, we can compare the performance of companies who invest in learning with those who do not. Studies have shown that companies who invest significantly in learning perform, on average, at least 15% better than their lower-investment competitors in the same industry. The American Society for Training and Development (ASTD) found that average companies spend an amount equivalent to about 2% of their total payroll on training; outstanding companies (when judged by business performance) spend 4% or more per year. Those companies that spend less than 2% tend to quickly become noncompetitive. Companies like GE, IBM and Ford Motor Company continue to reap the rewards of having invested heavily in learning over past decades.

But it is just not enough to simply throw money at learning. The money must be used judiciously and be required to return better business performance for its investment. And learning does not have to be expensive.

A good learning architecture identifies the learning offerings most necessary to the organization, and prioritizes them according to the expected return on investment. Then for each specific type of learning delivered, it is the task of the Chief Learning Officer (or someone else responsible for the learning budget) to find the most economical way to deliver that learning at the required quality level.

There are many ways to be frugal about learning. Courses or learning programs bought in quantity are always less expensive, if the need is great enough to justify the quantity. Eliminating overlap or duplication in learning offerings can also save significant amounts. Having internal leaders or experts teach can not only save money (after all, they are already on the payroll) but also improve the quality and relevance of the learning delivered. Techniques of distance learning enabled by advances in information technology can save huge amounts of money that would otherwise be spent on participant travel. It is not necessary to conduct learning in resorts or expensive hotels. And while a certain amount of social interaction is desirable to promote networking among participants, splashy high cost meals and social events do not contribute to the learning that is the purpose of getting people together.

Organizations today will be much more willing to offer and promote learning to their members if they can see that the learning is being delivered in the most cost-effective way possible. It is the responsibility of the CLO (or equivalent) to constantly show and remind line leadership that learning is being sourced and delivered at the lowest possible cost, given the quality level required or desired. In this, the CLO has to be a cost-conscious designer and deliverer of learning, and a constant reporter of learning's frugality to the line leadership (and the CFO). *Learning must be marketed.*

How to Build Your Own Learning Architecture

If you are part of an enlightened organization that wants to build a comprehensive, results-focused, cost-effective learning architecture, we reprise here the steps described earlier in the book.

1. Be certain that your organizational leadership is ready to promote and support learning. This cannot just be lip service, but both financial and role-modeled support. If you are not sure of their support, do not even begin to build a learning architecture, because it will become an empty façade and the

organization's members will lose their belief that the organization cares about their development.

2. Conduct a comprehensive learning needs analysis. Identify the learning that will most benefit the organization, and prioritize its components.

3. Design the most effective learning to address each identified learning need. Choose from classroom learning, distance learning, external programs, action learning, coaching, mentoring, computer-enabled learning, job mobility and any other pedagogy that will accomplish your learning objectives.

4. Carefully identify and choose the providers of each type of learning. They may be internal or external to your company or organization. Choose providers who specialize in the specific learning you want delivered; providers with plenty of experience in that subject or learning modality. Make sure that they are world-class—lesser quality learning is more expensive in the end. And poorly designed or delivered learning will not only embarrass you, but will set back the entire learning process in your organization.

5. Carefully identify and choose the recipients of the learning. Be sure they need the learning, first of all; and be certain their organizational performance warrants the investment you are about to make in them. Let learning be an earned privilege, not an entitlement.

6. Manage the delivery of learning with comprehensive care. Take personal responsibility for the quality of learning delivery. Oversee all important aspects of learning delivery—do not delegate this important responsibility.

7. Calculate both the cost and value delivered of learning. Use metrics that have face validity and reasonably approximate the value being derived from learning. Remember that valuing learning is an inexact science, and settle for approximations. On the cost side, carefully record all costs of learning, both direct and indirect (such as value of time spent).

8. Keep senior leadership constantly apprised of both the costs of learning and the value being derived (do not present one

without the other). Keep them involved by including them as presenters or teachers. Use them as advisors to the learning architecture and ask them to make suggestions to improve learning in the organization.

9. Providing continuous employee development opportunities helps attract and retain good talent. Let the world know how good your learning architecture is. Make use of your professional associations to tout your organization's learning. Get press coverage if you can. Use the added clout of better attraction and retention to justify the continuation and enhancement of learning in your organization.

10. Finally, do not allow your learning architecture to become stale, irrelevant or obsolete. Constantly review your architecture in light of what's happening in your competitive arena. Be sure it is always addressing the most important learning needs of your company or organization. And do not be afraid to put a "sunset" clause on every component of your architecture—if it becomes irrelevant or much less important, kill it. It is easy for learning architectures to become bloated and cost-ineffective over time if they are not constantly pruned. Periodic review keeps the learning architecture from becoming vulnerable to attack or discontinuation because it is not fulfilling its intended purpose.

Do all these things faithfully and you will have a learning architecture that is better than most. It will make a massive contribution to your organization's success over the short and long term, and become a source of pride for your organization's unique brand.

Adapt Don't Adopt

With today's emphasis on benchmarking to identify practices that work well for other organizations, it is tempting to merely adopt for your organization what works for someone else. In the area of learning, this is a mistake. Learning architectures are, by definition, grounded in the culture of their organization. They are not successfully transferable from one organization to another.

We have seen many attempts to graft successful learning architectures, like those of GE, IBM and Hewlett-Packard, onto other companies. These attempts are never fully successful, and usually fall far short of accomplishing the learning goals of the adopting organization. Successful learning structures like those mentioned have grown up in the nurturing soil of their host companies, with all the high-level support and cultural input necessary to make them so effective. These nurturing conditions are often absent in the adopting organization.

Instead of simply grafting another organization's learning architecture onto your own company, take pieces of perhaps several good architectures and adapt them for your own use. You may take a leadership learning process from here, a coaching model from there, a faculty source from yet another company; and amalgamate them all into a learning architecture that's right for your organization. There is nothing wrong with using good ideas that others have generated—in fact some companies say they will "steal shamelessly" any good idea they can use. It is not necessary to invent your learning architecture from scratch.

Here's where the skill of the CLO, or whoever fills that role, comes in. It is his or her job to study and become familiar with enough learning architectures of other companies to know what components of other architectures to cherry-pick. This is a time-consuming process that requires dedication to the task, and access to other organizations. The dedication part is relatively easy; it is the access part that is more difficult.

The best way to acquire access to the learning structures of other organizations is through the networks of learning professionals that connect with each other to share ideas about learning. Most of the members of these networks have responsibility for learning in their organizations. They may be based in companies, non- and not-for-profits, even academe. They may also be consultants who specialize in learning or writers on the topic. Some such networks are UNICON, The Learning Network and the Executive Leadership Development Network. Trade groups like the American Society for Training and Development (ASTD) and the Society for Human Resource Management (SHRM) can also be helpful. All of these networks can be reached by the Internet.

The point here is that a good CLO needs to take the time to find out what learning architectures exist, where they are and why they work in the organizations in which they are imbedded. Then it is his or her task to make use of the parts of other architectures that are particularly suited for their own organization and adapt those components for their own use. Every organization has special learning needs, and components taken from other organizations' architectures must be customized for these special uses. Again, the keyword here is adapt, not adopt.

How to Judge the Success of Your Learning Architecture

It is much easier to judge the effectiveness and efficiency of a learning architecture over time; harder to do in the short term. Companies that have been successful over many years, like GE, H-P, Royal Dutch Shell, Unilever, Colgate-Palmolive and Nestle can point to their learning architectures as the prime drivers of their success. They have completely assimilated a learning mindset into their cultures. They have used learning to attract, develop and retain the best employees available anywhere. They are constantly developing their intellectual human capital, causing it to appreciate over time, not depreciate as it does in so many lesser organizations. For organizations like these, it is easy to see how successful their learning architectures have become.

But what if your organization is younger than these examples, or your learning architecture is newer? How best to judge the quality and success of your learning architecture? Here are a few criteria:

1. People in your organization are excited to learn, and do so constantly.

2. Learning is available for almost any legitimate learning need.

3. People are motivated to self-nominate for learning; they seek it out, do not wait to be asked or for it to be directly offered.

4. People are attracted to your company or organization because of the help they get with their personal development, and the expectation they will develop themselves continually (they will not be seen as "odd" because they seek learning).

5. People will stay in your organization for the learning and development opportunities, which might not be available elsewhere.

6. People are constantly making suggestions about how to enrich or enlarge their learning opportunities.

7. Your organization quickly acquires a reputation "on the street" as a learning organization.

8. Senior leadership recognizes that they are getting excellent value for the dollars they invest in learning—an exceptional rate of return.

9. Senior leadership knows that all the most important learning needs in the organization are being met, and at a high quality level.

10. Your learning architecture is a capable tool and support system for advancing your organization's strategy. All of its parts are seen to have a useful purpose; there are no parts of the architecture that add little or no value.

If your learning architecture meets these criteria, no matter how new it may be, you have done a good job of designing and managing it.

Importance of Networking for Learning Professionals

The job of Chief Learning Officer can be a lonely one. It is easy to get so caught up in the day-to-day tasks that one loses sight of the learning world outside of one's own organization. The best way to combat this potential handicap is by belonging to several networks of organizational learning professionals. Earlier we mentioned UNICON, the Learning Network, the Executive Leadership Development Network and ASTD. None of these is completely exclusive, although some are easier to join than others. It is well worth the effort to seek membership with these organizations. The reinforcement that learning professionals get from these organizations can be most useful when learning program designs are being questioned or approaches to learning are being challenged. They are a great source of new ideas for learning, and may offer solutions to learning problems.

Onward and Upward with Learning

We hope this book has been a source of useful ideas about organizational and individual learning. As we move forward in the new millennium, increasing human intellectual capital becomes ever more important to organizations of all kinds. At the center of these efforts is the Chief Learning Officer, or his or her counterpart. If you are fortunate enough to be in this role, you are fortunate indeed, because your ideas and efforts will spell the difference for your organization being just an average performer, or being a competitive winner. What an exciting challenge for all of us!

Dr. Warren Wilhelm
January, 2003

Reference List

Argyris, C., Teaching Smart People How to Learn, *Harvard Business Review*, May-June 1991, 99–109.

Drucker, Peter, *12 Key Challenges for the 1990s*, CSC Index, Cambridge, MA, 1991.

Fulmer, R. and M. Goldsmith, *The Leadership Investment*, Amacom, New York, 2001.

Hampden-Turner, C. and A. Trompenaars, *The Seven Cultures of Capitalism: Value Systems for Creating Wealth in the United States, Japan, Germany, France, Britain, Sweden, and The Netherlands*, Currency/Doubleday, New York, 1993.

Handy, C. B., *The Age of Unreason*, Harvard Business School Press, Boston, MA, 1990.

———., *The Age of Paradox*, Harvard Business School Press, Boston, MA, 1994.

Johnson, B., *Polarity Management: Identifying and Managing Unsolvable Problems*, HRD Press, Amherst, MA, 1992.

Leadership Development Survey, Executive Development Associates, Crested Butte, CO, 1999.

Kirkpatrick, D. L., *Evaluating Training Programs: The Four Levels*, Berrett-Koehler Publishers, San Francisco, CA, 1994.

Miles, R. H., *Leading Corporate Transformation: An Executive Briefing*, Jossey-Bass, San Francisco, 1997.

O'Toole, J., *Leading Change: Overcoming the Ideology of Comfort and the Tyranny of Custom*, Jossey-Bass, San Francisco, CA, 1995.

Rossett, A., Training and Organization Development: Separated at Birth, *Training*, April, 1996, 53–59.

Senge, P., *The Fifth Discipline: The Art and Practice of the Learning Organization*, Doubleday/Currency, New York, 1990.

Shapiro, E. C., *Fad Surfing in the Boardroom: Reclaiming the Courage to Manage in the Age of Instant Answers*, Addison-Wesley Publishing, Reading, MA, 1995.

Tichy, N. The Teachable Point of View: A Primer, *Harvard Business Review*, May–April, 1999, 82–83.

Treacy, M. and F. Wiersema, *The Discipline of Market Leaders: Choose Your Customers, Narrow Your Focus, Dominate Your Market*, January, 1997.

Trompenaars, A. and C. Hampden-Turner, *Riding the Waves of Culture: Understanding Cultural Diversity in Global Business*, 2nd Ed., McGraw-Hill, New York, 1998.

Ulrich, D., M. Von Glinow and T. Jick, High-Impact Learning: Building and Diffusing Learning Capability, *Organizational Dynamics*, Winter, 1993, 52–66.

Ulrich, D., J. Zenger and N. Smallwood, *Results-Based Leadership*, Harvard Business School Press, 1999.

Wilhelm, W., Accelerated Leader Development, *Leader to Leader*, Summer, 2001, 16–19.

Wilhelm, W., Learning from Past Leaders, Chapter 22 in *The Leader of the Future*, The Drucker Foundation, Jossey-Bass, San Francisco, CA, 1996.

Wilhelm, W., Total Learning Architecture: A Major Competitive Advantage, *Human Resource Professional*, March/April, 1999.

Yeung, A., D. Ulrich, S. Nason and M. Von Glinow, *Organizational Learning Capability: Generating and Generalizing Ideas with Impact,* Oxford University Press, New York, 1998.

Zigarmi, P., D. Zigarmi and K. Blanchard, *Leadership and the One Minute Manager: Increasing Effectiveness Through Situational Leadership,* 1985.

About the Author

Dr. Warren Wilhelm lives in Albuquerque, New Mexico with his wife Judy and three teenage children. He consults to organizations of all kinds in the areas of leadership development, human resource management and organizational change. He is president of Global Consulting Alliance and teaches human resource management in the executive masters program at Thunderbird, The American Graduate School of International Management headquartered in Phoenix, Arizona.

This book was written because there are constantly new professionals moving into jobs that require them to build learning architectures in organizations, and few opportunities exist for them to learn how to do it. The author's hope is that this compendium of information on the topic will be a kick-starter for those professionals in their daunting task.

Organizations all over the world have a serious scarcity of capable employees and leaders. If this book helps in even a small way to relieve the shortage, it will have achieved its primary objective; and the world we all inhabit will be more accomplished and better led.